Thinking about Capitalism
Part I

Professor Jerry Z. Muller

THE TEACHING COMPANY ®

PUBLISHED BY:

THE TEACHING COMPANY
4840 Westfields Boulevard, Suite 500
Chantilly, Virginia 20151-2299
1-800-TEACH-12
Fax—703-378-3819
www.teach12.com

Copyright © The Teaching Company, 2008

Printed in the United States of America

This book is in copyright. All rights reserved.

Without limiting the rights under copyright reserved above,
no part of this publication may be reproduced, stored in
or introduced into a retrieval system, or transmitted,
in any form, or by any means
(electronic, mechanical, photocopying, recording, or otherwise),
without the prior written permission of
The Teaching Company.

ISBN 1-59803-512-6

Jerry Z. Muller, Ph.D.

Professor of History, The Catholic University of America

Jerry Z. Muller is Professor of History at The Catholic University of America, where he has taught since 1984. He received his B.A. from Brandeis University and his M.A. and Ph.D. from Columbia University. He has been a fellow of the American Academy in Berlin; the Rockefeller Foundation Center in Bellagio, Italy; the Olin Foundation; the Bradley Foundation; and the American Council of Learned Societies.

Professor Muller is the author of *The Mind and the Market: Capitalism in Modern European Thought* (published in paperback as *The Mind and the Market: Capitalism in Western Thought*), which was cowinner of The Historical Society's Donald Kagan Best Book in European History Prize. He is also the author of *Adam Smith in His Time and Ours: Designing the Decent Society* and *The Other God That Failed: Hans Freyer and the Deradicalization of German Conservatism*.

Professor Muller is also editor of *Conservatism: An Anthology of Social and Political Thought from David Hume to the Present*. His many articles and essays have appeared in scholarly journals as well as in *Foreign Affairs*, *The New Republic*, *The Times Literary Supplement*, *The Wall Street Journal*, and *The Wilson Quarterly*.

Table of Contents
Thinking about Capitalism
Part I

Professor Biography i
Course Scope 1
Lecture One   Why Think about Capitalism? 4
Lecture Two   The Greek and Christian Traditions 19
Lecture Three   Hobbes's Challenge to the Traditions 33
Lecture Four   Dutch Commerce and National Power 47
Lecture Five   Capitalism and Toleration—Voltaire 62
Lecture Six   Abundance or Equality—
                     Voltaire vs. Rousseau 77
Lecture Seven   Seeing the Invisible Hand—Adam Smith 91
Lecture Eight   Smith on Merchants, Politicians, Workers 106
Lecture Nine   Smith on the Problems
                     of Commercial Society 120
Lecture Ten   Smith on Moral and Immoral Capitalism 135
Lecture Eleven   Conservatism and Advanced
                     Capitalism—Burke 149
Lecture Twelve   Conservatism and Periphery
                     Capitalism—Möser 164
Timeline 179
Glossary 186
Biographical Notes 190
Bibliography 204

Thinking about Capitalism

Scope:

This course is designed to help us think about capitalism, not only as an economic system, but in terms of its moral, political, and cultural effects. Does the spread of the market—both across geographical borders and into more and more regions of our lives—make us better off or worse? What effect does it have on personal development, on the family, and on collective identities? Is economic growth desirable, and if so, what sorts of policies are most conducive to economic development?

This course focuses on the response to such questions by major European and American thinkers from the 17th through the 20th centuries, with a view to casting light on recurrent and perennial issues in thinking about capitalism. Placing each thinker in historical context, it provides an overview of the development of modern capitalism and of the cultural and political reactions to it. Exploring the historical roots of thinking about what has come to be called "globalization," the course provides perspectives on capitalism that are not typically encountered in economics courses or on the business pages of newspapers—perspectives drawn from a variety of political, disciplinary, and national points of view.

We begin by examining the two main premodern traditions that formed the backdrop against which modern intellectuals thought about commerce: the civil republican tradition (a legacy of ancient Greece and Rome) and the Christian tradition. Both traditions were suspicious of commerce. One form of commerce, the lending of money at interest, was viewed as a sin by the Catholic Church. This important economic function was relegated to the Jews, who were seen as beyond the brotherhood of the faithful, with later consequences that we trace in the course.

In the 17th century, in reaction to an era of religiously based civil war, Thomas Hobbes and other thinkers called into question the ideal of a polity dominated by religious ideals. They advanced a view of the world based upon the pursuit of worldly happiness, and they explored the potentially positive role of self-interest. At the same time, the rise of Holland led European thinkers and policymakers to a new emphasis on the link between commerce and national power.

Through an examination of the career of Voltaire, we explore the rise of intellectuals as shapers of public opinion, a rise made possible by the market for print. We examine Voltaire's arguments for the connection between commerce and toleration, and his debate with Jean-Jacques Rousseau over whether the rise in material well-being is conducive to happiness and morality.

Four lectures present a nuanced view of the ideas of Adam Smith, author of *The Wealth of Nations*, perhaps the most influential work ever written about capitalism. Smith explained how a competitively structured market could channel self-interest into a higher level of material well-being for all. But he also pointed to the difficulties of creating and maintaining a competitive market economy, to some of its intrinsic dangers, and to the role of government in combating these dangers. He offered a balance sheet that tallied the moral and immoral sides of contemporary capitalism. In a later lecture, we look at the work of a sympathetic critic, Alexander Hamilton, and why he believed that the free trade policies Smith advocated were inappropriate for the new United States, and for any nation seeking to emerge from what we would now call "underdevelopment." We look at the tensions between conservatism and capitalism in the work of the late 18th-century thinkers Edmund Burke and German writer Justus Möser.

In the 19th century, we examine the arguments of Hegel about the link between commerce and modern individuality, and the role of the state in making both possible. We explore Alexis de Tocqueville's reflections on the pitfalls and possibilities offered by capitalism as he encountered it in America. Two lectures devoted to Karl Marx examine his cultural criticism of the nature of work under capitalism and the reasons for his prediction that the ongoing misery of the new industrial working class would lead to class conflict and the end of capitalism. Marx's contemporary, British critic Matthew Arnold, provides a conception of cultural criticism that is not antipathetic to markets but is wary of applying market criteria to other areas of life.

A series of lectures explores the turn of the century debates between German social theorists Ferdinand Tönnies, Georg Simmel, Max Weber, and Werner Sombart on the relationship of capitalism to community, individuality, rationalization, and religion.

Joseph Schumpeter's conception of capitalism as "creative destruction," in which entrepreneurial activity creates dynamism but invites resentment and reaction, is the subject of another lecture. We examine the early 20th-century debate between Lenin and others on the relationship of capitalism to imperialism and to war.

After a brief look at the policies adopted by Lenin's Bolshevik government in the new Soviet Union, we look at a spectrum of reactions to the crises of capitalism in the interwar era, and the new analyses to which they gave rise, from intellectuals associated with fascism (Carl Schmitt and Hans Freyer), neoliberalism (Ludwig von Mises and Friedrich von Hayek), and ironic conservatism (Schumpeter). Then we explore the rise of welfare-state capitalism, including its intellectual origins in social democracy, Christianity, and in the new liberalism represented by John Maynard Keynes. We explore the varieties of postwar welfare-state capitalism (as explained by Gøsta Esping-Andersen) before turning to its foremost critics from the left (Herbert Marcuse) and the right (Hayek).

In the 1970s, American sociologist Daniel Bell argued that capitalism was developing into a postindustrial society, yet he thought there was a risk that the character traits promoted by contemporary culture and by the market itself might undermine the system. The economic stagnation of the era led to the growth of analyses of the tensions between democracy and capitalist economic growth, which we explore in the work of James M. Buchanan and Mancur Olson.

A lecture on the family and the market shows how each of these institutions continues to transform the other, and explores the trade-offs between household labor, paid labor, and familial consumption. Later lectures examine contemporary globalization in historical perspective, the link between capitalism and nationalism as explained by Ernest Gellner, the varieties of contemporary capitalism, and finally the intrinsic tensions of capitalism and the reasons it has outlasted its competitors.

By the end of the course, listeners should have a broad sense of the history of modern capitalism, an acquaintance with what Matthew Arnold called "the best that has been thought and said" about capitalism, and an arsenal of concepts with which to think about contemporary developments.

Lecture One
Why Think about Capitalism?

Scope:

This course provides a historical introduction to thinking about how capitalism works, and about its political, moral, and cultural prerequisites and effects. For the most part, our approach is historical, trying to understand what the great debates of the past were about, with an eye to thinking about their current resonance and ramifications. We provide a working definition of "capitalism," discuss the history of the term, and learn why it is plausible to argue that societies first became capitalist in the 17th or 18th centuries.

Outline

I. Capitalism is a central phenomenon of modern life, and as intellectually and morally reflective people, we should be interested in getting some critical perspective on it.
   A. This series of lectures is an attempt to convey what Matthew Arnold called "the best that has been thought and said" about capitalism, in order to provide fresh perspectives upon it.
   B. I am a Professor of History at The Catholic University of America and have a particular interest in intellectual history (i.e., the history of ideas and of intellectuals).
   C. The premise of this series of lectures is that capitalism is too important and complex a subject to be left to economists because it involves a great deal more than what we typically think of as "economic."

II. The course sets out to convey a variety of ways of thinking about capitalism.
   A. It examines capitalism from various political and disciplinary perspectives, and from thinkers who transcend normal political and disciplinary boundaries.
   B. The course focuses on how capitalism has been analyzed, interpreted, and evaluated by intellectuals, rather than by major capitalists.
   C. In order to understand their concerns and to appreciate their insights, the lectures put them in their historical contexts.

III. Capitalism has changed over time.
   A. The capitalism of the 17th and 18th centuries focused on the importation to Europe of new goods from overseas and on new means of production, such as cottage industry based on a greater division of labor.
   B. In the 18th century, there was a financial revolution connected to the rise of international trading companies and the rise of a market for government bonds. There was also a consumer revolution, at least in England and northwestern Europe.
   C. In the 19th century and well into the 20th century, it was industrial factory production that moved to center stage.
   D. The 19th century saw the rise of several new institutions with tremendous ramifications for the development of capitalism, including the limited liability corporation, the development of the bureaucratic corporation, and the development of trade unions and labor parties.
   E. In the course of the 20th century, advanced capitalist societies moved from an industrial economy to one increasingly focused on what we've come to call "services."

IV. The term "capitalism" is relatively new, though as often happens in the history of ideas, the phenomenon existed long before the term, and under a variety of labels.
   A. It was originally a political slogan, a term coined by socialists who sought to stigmatize the phenomenon.
   B. The term came into more neutral, social scientific usage at the beginning of the 20th century.

V. Like most concepts in the social sciences, "capitalism" is an ideal type—a model, an abstraction from experience that helps us grasp the key elements under consideration and their relationship to one another.
   A. The first of those elements is private property. Usually, private property depends on the existence of governmental power that is able to protect property.
   B. The second element is exchange between legally free individuals, as opposed to serfdom or slavery, in which labor is extracted by political superiority.

- C. The third element is that capitalism is a system in which the production and distribution of goods operate primarily through the market mechanism, rather than by custom or common decision of any sort.
- D. This is a model from which there have historically been many variations and even divergences.

VI. The question of when capitalism began has no discrete answer.
- A. There was a good deal of trade in the Middle Ages; indeed, historians speak of a commercial revolution of the Middle Ages, from about 1100 to 1300. But most households continued to consume most of the things that they produced, and to produce most of what they consumed.
- B. It is only in the 18th century that in the most advanced parts of Europe, the majority of people came to buy most of the things they needed, and to buy those things, they took to selling most of what they produced, rather than using it themselves.
- C. This meant the growth of market-oriented households.

VII. Households became more market-oriented in a variety of ways.
- A. One way was through agricultural specialization, in which goods are produced not for household consumption, but with an eye toward selling them to others.
- B. Another way was through cottage industry, in which family members within the home produce goods for sale.
- C. Another way was through wage labor: working for others to gain money, rather than working in the household itself or taking more leisure time.
- D. In turn, households increasingly purchased items that in the past would have been made at home because it was more efficient for them to do so.
- E. They increasingly lived in a commercial society, in which, as Adam Smith put it, everyone was a merchant to some degree or another.

Suggested Reading:

Braudel, *Civilization and Capitalism 15th-18th Century*, vol. 2, 237–239 (deals with the history of the term "capitalism").

Hirschman, "Rival Views of Market Society."

Questions to Consider:
1. What connotations does the term "capitalism" have to you, or in the circles in which you travel? Do you know others who hold a different view? If so, how does their definition or conception of capitalism differ from yours?
2. In our society, capitalism is often regarded as the purview of economists. What sorts of important questions about capitalism do economists (or the business pages of the newspaper) typically ignore?

Lecture One—Transcript
Why Think about Capitalism?

Capitalism. Few phenomena are more central to our lives, and as intellectually and morally reflective people, we should be interested in trying to get some critical perspective on it. That's what this course of lectures is intended to do. One of the thinkers we'll be looking at, Matthew Arnold, the British poet and cultural critic, defined culture as:

> a pursuit of our total perfection by means of getting to know, on all the matters which most concern us, the best which has been thought and said in the world; and, through this knowledge, turning a stream of fresh and free thought upon our stock notions and habits.

This series of lectures, you could say, is an attempt to convey the best that's been thought and said about capitalism in order to provide you with some fresh perspectives on it.

My name is Jerry Muller. I'm a Professor of History at The Catholic University of America, in Washington, DC. I'm primarily an intellectual historian by trade. That is to say, I'm concerned with the history of ideas, with the people who articulate ideas, people that we usually call "intellectuals"—writers, philosophers, social scientists—people who try to think about how things hang together, how institutions and traditions are related to one another. I'm interested in the ideas that they held, in how they came to hold those ideas, and in the influence that their ideas had over others.

I come from an entrepreneurial family. My father is an entrepreneur, my grandfather was, his father was as well. When I was growing up, I worked in a number of family businesses, but I didn't want to go into business. I wanted to be an intellectual, to learn about and reflect on the interconnection of things. But I certainly understood that capitalism was something that was worth thinking about, and thinking about how it's connected to many other things.

That's what I've been studying for some time now, and in these lectures I want to share with you some of those connections. The theme of this course is "thinking about capitalism," and I mean that in two senses. First of all, how major intellectuals in Europe and the United States have thought about capitalism, and how *you* might consider thinking about capitalism.

When people come to think about capitalism, their first inclination is, perhaps, to turn to the business pages of the newspaper, or to turn to economists to explain it to them. In the business pages we can read about which companies are more profitable and which are less so; what products people are buying and which ones they've stopped buying; the prospects for employment, for inflation, and so on. Economists tend to focus on how one element of market-related activity is related to other elements—how money supply affects inflation, say, or how interest rates affect investment and consumer spending.

The premise of this series of lectures is that there is a lot more to capitalism than that—that capitalism is too important and complex to be left to the economists. That's because capitalism involves a great deal more than what we typically think of as economic. It's a system, or rather a variety of systems, by which people compete and cooperate with one another; through which they try to satisfy their goals, their needs, their wants; and through which new goals, and new needs, and new wants are constantly being created.

Capitalism is a system that has political prerequisites, and it has political effects. It's a system that has cultural effects and just what those effects are is a topic that's been under intense debate for several hundred years now. In fact, almost every aspect of the way we think about ourselves as individuals and as groups is influenced by capitalism.

Take something that might seem to be entirely beyond the realm of capitalism: our families, the size and shape of our families. Why is it that when capitalism first develops, families tend to get larger in size (that is to say, people tend to have more children)? But then, as capitalism develops further, people tend to have fewer children, despite the fact that they're better off. Or, take the way in which capitalism is related to the larger groups with which we identify, to classes and nations.

As you will see, some thinkers maintain that capitalism tends to break down national barriers, while others have argued that there's a close connection between capitalism and the development of the modern nation-state.

Capitalism also influences the way in which we define ourselves as individuals by our chosen interests. The fact that we might think of ourselves as a jazz aficionado, for example, is linked to our shared appreciation and consumption of concerts and recorded music, and those connections link us to others around the country and perhaps around the world. That's made possible by the commodification of music; that is to say, the fact that musical performances can be bought and sold in the capitalist marketplace and that some people can therefore specialize in making the sort of music that we want to listen to, or writing the sorts of novels that we want to read, and so on.

As I studied modern intellectual history, I found that key thinkers in the United States and in Europe, going back at least to the 18th century, were interested in the development of capitalism and understood that it was central to understanding the modern world. I found that was true not only of thinkers who we usually think of in this regard, like Adam Smith or Karl Marx, but also writers like Voltaire in the 18th century, or Matthew Arnold in the 19th, or philosophers like Hegel—figures who we don't usually think of as having had much to say about these matters.

As I came to study some of the thinkers more carefully, I found that thinkers like Adam Smith and Joseph Schumpeter, who are usually thought of as economists, actually had a much wider range of concerns than is characteristic of contemporary economics. So what I've set out to do is to lay out for you a variety of ways of thinking about capitalism, a kind of intellectual banquet, or a smorgasbord perhaps.

We'll be looking at capitalism from a variety of political perspectives, from those of protectionists and free traders, liberals, conservatives, socialists, fascists, communists. We'll also be looking at capitalism from a variety of disciplinary perspectives, some drawn from economics, some from one or another form of philosophy, some from sociology, some from political science. But the truth is many of the most stimulating perspectives are from thinkers who actually transcend disciplinary boundaries and often transcend political boundaries as well.

Not only do I hope to convey to you a variety of ways of thinking about capitalism, but in the last lectures of the course I want to emphasize the variety of contemporary capitalist systems. It's sometimes said that the decline of communism in the Soviet Union, in Eastern Europe, and in China in the last decade and a half have brought about the victory of capitalism. That's a half-truth. Actually, there is a variety of forms of contemporary capitalism. Some are more entrepreneurial and dynamic, some are less so but with virtues of their own, some of them are in democratic capitalist societies, some are in nondemocratic capitalist societies.

Our focus will be on how capitalism has been analyzed, interpreted, and evaluated by intellectuals. But why, you might ask, why don't you tell us what capitalists thought about capitalism? Why not focus on the line of great capitalists from, say, Josiah Wedgwood in the 18th century, the great pottery manufacturer; through Werner von Siemens, the founder of the German Siemens engineering firm; through Andrew Carnegie, John D. Rockefeller, and Henry Ford. The answer is—I'm afraid it wouldn't be very enlightening—it's not that these men were unintelligent or lacking in cleverness. On the contrary, they were both intelligent and clever. They were very good at what they did, but they were imminently practical men: focused, driven, expert in their areas of concentration. But practical men are rarely reflective men. They rarely have the time, the knowledge, or the inclination to reflect on the broader structures of which they are a part. So just as you wouldn't turn to Joe DiMaggio to explain the cultural and economic significance of baseball, you'd be ill-advised to turn to business leaders to understand the larger contexts and ramifications of business. Trying to put things in their larger contexts, to think about their deeper roots and their broader ramifications, that's precisely what intellectuals do for a living. Indeed, that's what makes them intellectuals, as opposed to just specialists in one or another particular field.

In order to understand their concerns and to appreciate their insights, we'll be putting the insights of these intellectuals into their historical contexts to see what capitalism meant at the time, and what its main institutions were.

There must be some common set of characteristics in order to be able to talk about capitalism. The nature of capitalism has certainly changed over time. The capitalism of the 17th and 18th centuries, for example, was focused on the one hand on the importation into Europe of new goods from overseas—goods that began as luxuries but that soon came to be perceived as necessities that everyone needed, like sugar, coffee, and tea—and on the other hand in the 17th and 18th centuries we have the development of new means of production, such as cottage industry (in which people manufactured various parts of larger processes in their homes): so a kind of process of production based on a greater division of labor.

As we'll see, there was a financial revolution in the 18th century as well that was connected to the rise of international trading companies, as well as to the rise of a market for government bonds. There was also a consumer revolution in the 18th century—at least there was in England and in northwestern Europe—and that consumer revolution formed the background of Adam Smith's *The Wealth of Nations*.

In the 19th century and well into the 20th, it was industrial factory production that moved to center stage of capitalism. And there was the rise in the course of the 19th century of several new institutions with tremendous ramifications for the development of capitalism—for example, the limited liability corporation, which allowed far more people to participate in the ownership of companies. In the 19th century, there was the development of the bureaucratic corporation, in which ownership and management of the firm were increasingly divorced from one another.

And in the course of the later 19th century, there was the development of trade unions—and eventually labor parties that fought to increase the economic and political power of the working classes. And then, in the course of the 20th century, capitalism was repeatedly transformed again as advanced capitalist societies moved from an industrial economy to an economy increasingly focused on what we've come to call "services," which involves everything from education and health care to the means of entertainment.

We'll be looking at the ideas of past intellectuals about capitalism in their historical contexts. But our inquiry isn't intended to be just antiquarian. We're not just focused on the past for its own sake. We'll also be looking at their ideas about capitalism with an eye towards the ongoing relevance of their insights.

Some lectures will focus on changing developments in capitalism as an economic and political phenomenon. We'll look, for example, at how at the beginning of the capitalist era, Holland became a model of how commercial power and political power were increasingly intertwined. Towards the end of the course we'll be looking at some of the transformations being brought about today by what's come to be called "globalization."

Most lectures will focus on one or another individual thinker. There are some thinkers that are so central to thinking about capitalism that we'll be devoting more than one lecture to them. We'll devote several lectures to Adam Smith, who probably did more than any other thinker to explain the functioning of the capitalist market, how a free market could lead to increased production and declining prices for consumer goods in the way that benefited the great mass of consumers. That's the main concern of his book *The Wealth of Nations*.

But Smith was also remarkably acute about the ways in which the pursuit of self-interest would lead people to try to prevent free competition, to benefit themselves as individuals and groups at the expense of the public interest. Smith also pointed to some of the intrinsic dangers of a commercial society, to the way in which it could lead to a kind of cultural degradation. He also looked at forms of capitalism that were harmful or morally evil, like slavery. So we'll be devoting a good deal of attention to Adam Smith.

We'll devote two lectures to the most influential modern critics of capitalism, that is to say, to Karl Marx and his collaborator, Friedrich Engels. We'll look at their cultural criticisms of capitalism and their critique of the degradation of work that they thought capitalism was bringing about. We'll devote a couple of lectures to the early 20th-century German social scientist Max Weber, who explored both the relationship between capitalism and religion and the relationship of capitalism to other key aspects of the modern world, like science and bureaucracy. We'll devote a good deal of attention to Joseph Schumpeter, whose main works appeared from 1911 to 1945, because he had such stimulating things to say not only about the sources of capitalist dynamism, but about the relationship between capitalism and so many other phenomena, from imperialism to the changing shape of the family.

So most lectures will focus on one or another individual thinker, but other lectures will focus on some key debate in which a number of thinkers took opposite sides. We'll look at the debate between Voltaire and Rousseau in the 18th century about luxury, a debate that as you will see leads us to the question of capitalism and inequality.

We'll look at the late 18th- and early 19th-century debate between Alexander Hamilton and Thomas Jefferson about whether the government of the United States ought to try to transform the new nation into an industrial society, an argument that continues to echo in discussions of how economically backward societies should try to catch up, what we now call "development economics."

We'll be looking at the debate between the late 19th-century German social scientists, Ferdinand Tönnies and Georg Simmel, about the relationship between capitalism, community, and individuality. Should we understand capitalism primarily as a destroyer of traditional communities or as creating new sorts of communities—communities that allow for a greater degree of individuality—or the debate on capitalism and its relationship to imperialism, a debate that pitted, among others, Vladimir Lenin against Joseph Schumpeter?

As you can see, these are not the sorts of questions typically addressed by contemporary economists or typically addressed in the business pages, but they are questions that morally aware people might want to consider.

What is capitalism? How should we define it? Before we try to come up with a working definition, let's turn our attention for a moment to the history of the word. The term "capitalism" is relatively new, though as often happens in the history of ideas, the phenomenon existed long before the term. It existed under a variety of other labels. Originally, "capitalism," the term, was really a political slogan, a term coined by socialists who sought to stigmatize the phenomenon. Karl Marx never used the noun "capitalism," but he did write about the "capitalist system of production," and though others had made use of it before Marx, it was really Marx who gave the term wider currency. And for Marx, the term "the capitalist system" had a clearly polemical meaning. It was made to indicate that the system worked on behalf of those who had money and who invested that money, at the expense of everyone else.

The term came into a more neutral, social scientific usage at the beginning of the 20th century, when the German sociologist Werner Sombart entitled his book *Modern Capitalism* in 1902. Two years later, another German sociologist, Max Weber, published the first part of his famous essay, "The Protestant Ethic and the 'Spirit' of Capitalism." After that, people started to use the term "capitalism" in a more value-neutral sense; that is to say, the term was used both by people who approved of capitalism and those who didn't.

But well before the word "capitalism" was in use, people were using a variety of other words to designate more or less the same phenomenon. Adam Smith, for example, writing in 1776, spoke of "commercial society," by which he meant something very close to capitalism. Like most concepts in the social sciences, capitalism is an ideal type. It's a kind of model. It's an abstraction from experience that helps us grasp key elements and their relationship to one another. So what are the key elements of capitalism?

The first is private property. That is by no means a simple concept. It actually implies a lot. You might think, isn't all property private, or at least isn't that the default position for property? The answer is no. In the real world, things belong to whoever has the power to take them unless there's a power that guarantees that other people won't take them. And so usually, private property depends on the existence of government power, that is to say, a power that is able to protect property from those who would like to steal it.

The second element of our model is that capitalism involves exchange between legally free individuals. That means that in a capitalist society when one person works for another, it's for wages, and when he exchanges something of value with someone else, it's for money. Well, you might say, what's the alternative? The historical alternative before the rise of modern capitalism was often a situation in which you worked for someone else because he was your political superior, or because he owned you. Much of Europe in the early modern period was still dominated by serfdom, in which lords owned land and exercised a good deal of direct control over the people on the land. The lord was entitled to a certain amount of unpaid work from his serfs, and he also had control over where a serf could live, and even who a serf could marry.

In eastern Europe and in Russia, serfdom persisted well into the mid-19th century. In western Europe, nobles were still entitled to various kinds of economic extractions from the peasants on their land up to the time of the French Revolution. In other parts of the world, including of course much of North and South America, there was slavery in the 17th and 18th centuries, that is to say, a situation in which some people owned others as property.

The third element of capitalism is that it's a system in which the production and distribution of goods operate primarily through the market mechanism. When we say that production and distribution operate through the market mechanism, we mean that prices are not set by custom, they're not set by government decision, they're not set by those who produce the goods; they're set by supply and demand. In other words, prices are not determined by anybody in particular. So our working definition of capitalism involves private property, exchange between legally free individuals, where production and distribution of goods occurs primarily through the market. But this is a sort of model from which in historical fact there have been many variations and divergences.

For example, the slave owners and slaves in the New World were very much a part of the international capitalist economy of their time. Most of the slaves in places like the Caribbean, Brazil, or in the colonies that later became the United States were purchased by their owners to grow crops that would be sold to others, crops like sugar or tobacco. Slavery, of course, is the opposite of legally free individuals, so this diverges from the model. The slave owners were legally free, but not the slaves. Some of you may think that we should either stick closely to the model and regard 18th- and 19th-century slavery as noncapitalist—the problem is, then, that we would fail to capture the close link between New World slavery and the larger Atlantic capitalist economy—or you might say we should drop the element of legally free labor from the model of capitalism. But that would leave out a key element of capitalism in most times and places.

It's best to keep the model of capitalism as characterized by the market mechanism, private property, exchange between legally free individuals, recognizing that this is a model from which reality has sometimes diverged.

When did capitalism begin? It's a difficult question. It's not the kind of question to which one can give a discrete answer, like when did the London Stock Exchange open its doors, or when was the first steam engine invented? Trade has been around for a very long time, but it's only relatively recently that a society based primarily on trade has come into existence. There has been bartering since the Stone Age. There was a good deal of trade in the ancient world, and in the Middle Ages. Indeed, historians speak of a commercial revolution of the Middle Ages, from about 1100 to about 1300.

But most households continued to consume most of the things that they themselves produced, and most households produced most of what they consumed. It's probably only in the 18th century that in the most advanced parts of Europe the majority of people came to buy most of the things they needed, and to buy those things, they took to selling most of what they produced rather than using it themselves.

One way of thinking about when a society can be said to become a capitalist society has to do with the distribution of time in the household. In the past, households had had contact with the market; that is to say, they had sold some goods that were produced in the household, but they were excess goods that were sold to try to supplement the household's income.

Now, with the rise of capitalism, one had the growth of market-oriented households, and households became market-oriented in a variety of ways. First of all, there was agricultural specialization. When people produce with an eye toward self-sufficiency, they tend to grow small amounts of a wide range of crops and animals, whereas when they produce with an eye toward the market, they tend to specialize, that is, to grow one or two goods that they're particularly good at with an eye toward selling those goods.

Another form of market orientation in the household is through cottage industry, that is to say, through devoting more family time to producing goods at home for sale in the marketplace, such as weaving textiles at home to be sold. Another version of this reorientation of household labor toward the market is, of course, wage labor—spending less time in the household and more time working for others in order to gain money rather than working in the household itself or taking more time as leisure time.

In turn, as people increasingly oriented themselves toward the market and oriented more of their time toward producing goods and labor in market activity, the other side of this was that people increasingly purchased items in the market that in the past would have been made at home: goods like beer, or furniture, or clothes, or needles, or pots and pans, or soap, and vinegar. They did so because it was more efficient for them to do so; that is to say, they could own a wider variety of desirable things than if they had to produce those things for themselves.

In order to buy these things from others, they worked harder, and they devoted more of their labor to making things that they could sell to others rather than to other household activities. They increasingly lived in a commercial society in which, as Adam Smith put it, everyone becomes a merchant to some degree or another. That's what European and American thinkers took to reflecting upon, and it's what we'll be reflecting upon in these lectures. And I hope that the lectures will encourage *you* to reflect upon it.

But the way in which European and American thinkers thought about a society in which everyone becomes a merchant to some degree was influenced by the stock of ideas that they had available to them. That stock of ideas came primarily from two older, premodern traditions: the legacy of ancient Greek thought and the legacy of Christianity.

As we'll see, neither of these traditions were disposed to think very highly of trade or the people that engaged in it.

Lecture Two
The Greek and Christian Traditions

Scope:

In thinking about how modern intellectuals have evaluated capitalism, we must keep in mind the premodern traditions that formed the backdrop against which modern thinkers developed their ideas. Commerce and moneymaking were regarded with suspicion in two of the great traditions of the West. In the civic republican tradition, which went back to ancient Greece, commerce was seen as ignoble, and the pursuit of economic self-interest was seen as a threat to civic virtue and the protection of the polity. In the Christian tradition, wealth was seen as promoting pride and hence impeding salvation, and the lending of money at interest was condemned as "usury." In medieval Europe, the stigmatized activity of lending money was permitted to Jews, who were seen as beyond the community of the saved.

Outline

I. How we interpret the world around us depends in good part on the categories that are available to us, and those come from the cultural traditions that are handed down to us.

   A. To understand the views of modern European and American thinkers, we have to keep in mind these older cultural traditions to see how they took issue with these new traditions or how they reformulated them under the new conditions of a more commercial society.

   B. Two of the main traditions that European and American intellectuals had available to them were very skeptical about commerce and moneymaking: Those were the traditions of civic republicanism and Christianity.

II. The civic republican tradition began in ancient Greece, was continued in classical Rome, and was revived in the Renaissance in Italy.

   A. It was formulated in Greek city-states that were republics (i.e., self-governing political entities).

- **B.** The problem for such republics was how to prevent getting conquered by other states, and how to prevent their republican self-government from degenerating into some form of dictatorial rule.
- **C.** The civic republican tradition stressed the importance of "virtue," understood as personal devotion to the republic through participation in its political life and a willingness to fight on its behalf.
- **D.** This ideal of "virtue" applied only to citizens, and citizens made up a minority of the population, excluding women, slaves, merchants, and artisans. The citizens of the city had to be economically independent, and citizens who used their votes or their government positions to enrich themselves were seen as corrupt.

III. The civic republican tradition was very suspicious of those who made their livelihood from trade.
- **A.** According to Aristotle, a well-governed city should not have citizens live a merchant's way of life because that way of life is "ignoble and contrary to virtue."
- **B.** He believed that commerce tended toward excess, and that merchants especially were subject to "pleonexia," translated as "overreaching" or "greediness."

IV. Christianity was the other great tradition that formed the cultural backdrop for modern European thinkers. It too was hostile to trade and to merchants, as well as to worldly acquisition in general.
- **A.** The Gospels warned that riches were a threat to salvation.
- **B.** The fathers of the church adhered to the classical assumption that because the material wealth of humanity was more or less fixed, the gain of some could only come at a loss to others.
- **C.** The church's attitude toward commerce began to change during the late Middle Ages, when the Scholastics formulated a less hostile view of trade.

- **D.** Thomas Aquinas defended private property and the dignity of labor, but his view of economic life was essentially hierarchical and static. Economic life, in his conception, should be ordered to provide the male head of the family with enough income to support his family according to the traditional standard of living.
- **E.** To try to get richer, then, was itself a sign of the sin of pride, and a danger to one's soul and to eternal salvation. We find echoes of this view after the Reformation as well, among both Dutch Calvinists and English Puritans.

V. Christian thinkers were vehemently opposed to usury (the taking of interest), on both biblical and philosophical grounds.
- **A.** The book of Deuteronomy allowed Jews to lend to non-Jews but prohibited Jews from lending with interest to each other.
- **B.** Aristotle had argued that the lending of money for profit was unjust because it was unnatural, because he viewed money as sterile.
- **C.** Usury was expressly forbidden by the Second Lateran Council of 1139. But this focus on usury was taking place at a time when the role of commerce in European life was starting to expand, and when people needed to borrow money.
- **D.** One method by which the church resolved this dilemma, beginning in the 12th century, was to prevent the evil of Christian usury by allowing Jews to engage in that forbidden economic activity.
- **E.** So began an association of moneymaking with the Jews, an association which would further taint attitudes toward commerce among Christians and which would survive in transmuted forms in the reflections of modern intellectuals.

Suggested Reading:

Muller, *The Mind and the Market*, chap. 1.

Rahe, *Republics Ancient and Modern*.

Noonan, *The Scholastic Analysis of Usury*.

Questions to Consider (and reconsider as the course progresses):
1. Is there a tension between public-spiritedness and capitalist market activity? Is there a role for civic virtue today?
2. Is there a conflict between being a Christian and functioning in a capitalist society?

Lecture Two—Transcript
The Greek and Christian Traditions

How we reflect on the world around us, how we interpret the world around us depends in good part on the categories that are available to us, and those categories come to us in part from cultural traditions that are handed down over time. Concepts are like flashlights: They call our attention to some aspect of reality, and they leave other aspects of reality in shadows. Concepts also have their own set of associations or evaluations that they're likely to call up. You can think of an intellectual tradition as a series of interrelated concepts, and as such, intellectual traditions tend to influence what elements of reality we see and how we evaluate those elements of reality.

To understand the views of modern European and American thinkers about capitalism, we have to keep in mind some older cultural traditions and how they tended to view and evaluate trade, finance, and consumption. We have to keep those in mind because we'll want to see how more modern European and American intellectuals sometimes took issue with those traditions, or how they reformulated those traditions under the new conditions of a more commercial society. We'll want to keep those older traditions in mind because they often form the backdrop of concepts, associations, and images that many of the readers that these thinkers were writing for would have in their minds.

Two of the main traditions that European and American intellectuals had available to them were very skeptical about commerce and about moneymaking and about consumption. Those were the traditions of civic republicanism and Christianity.

The civic republican tradition began in ancient Greece, was continued in classical Rome, and was revived during the Renaissance in Italy. It was originally formed in Greek city-states that were republics; that is, they were self-governing political entities. The problem for such republics, and the key problem for the civic republican tradition, was how to maintain themselves—how to prevent getting conquered by other states and how to prevent their republican self-government from degenerating into some form of dictatorial rule. This subject was explored in the great works of Greek philosophy in Plato, in Aristotle.

The civic republican tradition stressed the importance of virtue, where virtue was understood as personal devotion to the republic. When John F. Kennedy said, "Ask not what your country can do for you; ask what you can do for your country," he was reminding us of this civic republican ideal. And what you were supposed to do for your country, if you were a citizen, was two things above all.

First of all, you had to be prepared to fight for it, and second, you had to take a role in governing. You had to devote a good deal of time to public affairs in discussing how the city should be run. You had to be prepared to fight for it because these city-states were often at war with other city-states, and defeat meant the end of self-government for your city.

The ideal of virtue applied only to citizens, and citizens made up a minority of the population. Only adult males could be citizens. Indeed, the root of the word "virtue" is *vir*. That is Latin for "male," as in "virile." So citizenship was only open to adult males, and most males in the Greek city-states or in the later Roman Republic were not citizens. Many of them were slaves, or they were artisans without the status of citizens. To be a citizen meant to be the head of an economically self-sufficient household. Indeed, that's what the word "economy" originally meant. It was the science of a self-sufficient household. It was what we would call "home economics."

The free citizen was not supposed to have to devote himself very much to economic activity beyond managing his estate, where most of the work would be done by slaves or by artisans. The virtuous citizen was also supposed to be magnanimous, that is to say, large-minded, and to be concerned with making a living was considered to be small-minded. But that meant that virtue was only possible for those who didn't have to work to make a living because others were making it for them. The great fear within the civic republican tradition was corruption—that people would use their government positions to enrich themselves as individuals rather than looking out for the welfare of the city. That could lead to the decline of the city. So citizens of the city had to be economically independent, and citizens who used their votes, or their government positions, to enrich themselves were seen as corrupt. The civic republican tradition was very suspicious of those who actually made their livelihood from trade as opposed to farming on the land or owning slaves who farmed the land.

As Aristotle puts it, "In the city that is most finely governed, the citizens should not live a vulgar or a merchant's way of life, for this sort of [way of] life is ignoble and contrary to virtue." Why was Aristotle so suspicious of commerce, that is to say, buying and selling in order to make money? Because he argued the pursuit of money has no obvious natural end to it. It has no stopping point, and it tends toward excess.

If you were a farmer or you owned an estate that was worked by slaves, then you knew what you needed to have enough to feed, clothe, and support your family, your servants, and your slaves in the traditional manner, and you would produce enough to try to do that. In other words, in such a situation, money existed as a means to provide for a known, limited, traditional standard of living. But if you were a merchant who supported himself by making money through buying and selling, how would you know when you had enough? Aristotle thought that the pursuit of wealth lacks any intrinsic limit, so it's prone to excess. He thought that that applied to everyone, but he thought that merchants were especially subject to this problem, a problem that he called "pleonexia," which could be translated as "overreaching," or "greediness."

So the civic republican tradition, which emphasized civic virtue, tended to look down on those who made a living through trade, and it provided a way of looking at the world that was suspicious of the political effects of commerce. As we'll see, by the 17th and 18th centuries, thinkers were developing the civic republican tradition in a direction that made it more compatible with commerce, but for now it's important to remember the suspicion and disdain for commerce in the civic republican tradition.

The other great tradition that formed the cultural backdrop for modern European thinkers was, of course, Christianity. If classical Greek and Roman thought was suspicious of trade and merchants, Christianity was downright hostile, at least in its earliest forms, that is to say, in the Gospels and in the church fathers who wrote in the early centuries after Jesus.

The Gospels warned shrilly and repeatedly that riches and the pursuit of riches were a threat to salvation. "Do not lay up for yourselves treasures on earth," Jesus is reported to have preached in his Sermon on the Mount, "For where your treasure is, there will your heart be also." Or, "You cannot serve God and mammon," he warned. And most famously, "It is easier for a camel to go through the eye of a needle than for a rich man to enter the kingdom of God," from the Gospel of Mark.

In Paul's letter to Timothy, he writes that "Those who want to get rich fall into temptation and a trap and into many foolish and harmful desires that plunge people into ruin and destruction. For the love of money is a root of all kinds of evil."

Closely intertwined with this disparagement of the pursuit of wealth was the suspicion of merchants and the pursuit of profit. Here, it's interesting to see how Christians interpreted a story from the Gospel of Matthew. Here's the story:

> Jesus entered the temple of God and drove out all who sold and bought in the temple, and he overturned the tables of the moneychangers and the seats of those who sold pigeons. He said to them, "It is written, 'My house shall be called a house of prayers,' but you [make] it a den of robbers."

Now it's not at all clear that in this story Jesus is, in fact, condemning merchants or money changers at all, only that he was condemning them for conducting their affairs in the temple. But that's not the way that most early Christian commentators read the story.

Referring to these verses, an early collection of church law, known as canons, declared that the profession of the merchant was scarcely ever agreeable to God, and the great collection of canon law, compiled by Gratian in the middle of the 12th century, encapsulated the church's suspicious view of commerce. Gratian condemned trade and its profits absolutely. He writes, "… the man who buys in order that he may gain by selling it again unchanged as he bought it. That man is of the buyers and sellers who are cast forth from God's Temple."

In the prayers for the Thursday before Easter; that is to say, the day before Good Friday, Christians traditionally recited a prayer that referred to Judas Iscariot as "that most vile of merchants," implying that other merchants were somewhat less vile.

The fathers of the church adhered to the classical assumption that since the material wealth of humanity was more or less fixed, the gain of some could only come at a loss to others. As St. Augustine put it, the greatest of the church fathers, "If one does not lose, the other does not gain."

The church's attitude toward commerce began to change during the later Middle Ages. Remember I mentioned earlier the commercial revolution of the Middle Ages that took place from about 1100 to 1300. During that period there was an increase in agricultural productivity. That made it possible for people to grow more than they needed to consume, and to take the surplus and sell it. That agricultural surplus also meant that more people could live without growing their own food, that is to say, that more people could live in towns and cities. That created a necessity for merchants—for the people who got the produce from the countryside to the towns, and moved goods that were produced in the cities and towns into the countryside.

The Christian theologians of the period, who we call Scholastics, now had to deal with this new, more commercial reality where there was more trade and more merchants. They could see that these merchants were providing a useful service in providing their customers with wares from distant places, and they recognized that merchants were entitled to some remuneration for this service. So they developed the doctrine of the just price, which meant the market price—the price that was set by supply and demand in the absence of fraud; that is to say, when the buyer knew what he was buying and wasn't being deceived by the merchant. The Scholastics formulated a less hostile view of trade.

The greatest of the Scholastics was Thomas Aquinas, who lived in the 13th century, so in the midst of this commercial revolution. Thomas defended the necessity of private property. He also valued work, including the sorts of nonagricultural work that went on in towns. He had a place for merchants in all of this, but not a very large one. His view of society was essentially a hierarchical one, a static one. In this regard he was typical of the mind-set of the Middle Ages. For Thomas, the basis of the social order was the family, an institution that he thought arose naturally from man's sexual desire, which could be controlled by channeling it into marriage, where it led to the propagation of the species. He thought that it was natural and appropriate for people to form a hierarchy of occupations, and for people in each occupation to organize themselves into professional associations that were known as "guilds," so there were guilds of shoemakers, of barrel makers, silversmiths, and so on. Belonging to a guild would typically be handed down from generation to generation.

So economic life, in Thomas's conception, should be ordered to provide the male head of the family with enough income to support his family. But what was enough? What was the right standard? The answer for Thomas, as for most medieval thinkers, was the customary standard, the standard that was traditional for people in a given position in the social hierarchy. In this conception of society, everyone ought to know his place. People were not supposed to aspire to change their place in society; that is to say, there was no conception of upward or downward social mobility.

A good society, then, was one in which every husband could support his family in the traditional manner. It was wrong to want more. It was wrong to want to move beyond the position in society into which God had put you. But though the Scholastics found a place for trade and for merchants, they still remained highly mistrustful of them. Merchants, the Scholastics thought, were more tempted than others by the sin of avarice: the desire to have more than one's fair share. And remember that for Thomas and other Scholastics, one's fair share was one's traditional share. The desire to improve one's social status, to move up on the social ladder, that was suspect.

To try to get richer, then, was itself a sign of the sin of pride; and a danger to one's soul; and a danger, therefore, to one's eternal salvation. We find echoes of this view after the Reformation as well. Protestant theologians tended to be less suspicious of trade, but they were no less convinced that the pursuit of riches threatened salvation. We find sermons on that theme, about the dangers of the pursuit of wealth among Dutch Calvinists, English Puritans, and in many protestant churches thereafter—including in the colonial United States, with people like Cotton Mather.

If medieval Christian thinkers were suspicious of the merchant who bought and sold goods in order to make a profit, they were absolutely hostile to merchants of money, that is to say, people who lent out money to make a profit from it in the form of interest. Lending money at interest was known as "usury," and usury was a sin. Nowadays the term "usury" is usually used to mean excessive interest, but in the Christian tradition, it meant any interest whatsoever.

What's so bad about lending out money at interest? The Scholastics got their hostile view of usury from two sources. One was a biblical source, from the book of Deuteronomy in the Hebrew Bible, where it says, "You may lend with interest to foreigners, but to your brother you may not lend with interest." The Jewish understanding of this verse was that Jews were forbidden to lend money at interest to their brothers, that is to say, to other Jews, and that this was a direct commandment to them from God. It didn't have wider ramifications.

The interpretation of this verse by the Catholic Scholastic theologians was that the lending of money at interest was always sinful. They argued that all Christians were brothers, and therefore they couldn't lend out money, and they cited the verse from Deuteronomy, but they also cited Aristotle. This is of course what the Scholastics tried to do, to combine the Old and New Testament with the Greek tradition, especially Aristotle. Aristotle had actually argued that the lending of money for profit was unjust because it was unnatural. Money, Aristotle says, is sterile. It can't produce more money, and therefore someone who uses his money to produce more money for himself in the form of interest was committing an unjust act.

The medieval Catholic Scholastics adopted this argument and asserted that the prohibition of usury was part of natural law; that is, it ought to apply to everyone. So the Scholastic view, the Catholic view, was that lending money at interest was unnatural, unjust, and sinful, and usury was expressly forbidden by the Second Lateran Council of 1139.

Now, this focus on usury was taking place at the very time when the role of commerce in European life was starting to expand. And where you have commerce, you have people who need to borrow money. Indeed, it's hard to have much commercial activity without the possibility of borrowing money. It's hard to get people to lend out money just out of the goodness of their hearts, so a mortal sin of theology became a mortal necessity of economic life. As one wit put it, "Those who engage in usury go to hell; those who fail to engage in usury fall into poverty."

One way by which the church resolved this dilemma between the sinfulness of usury and the necessity of moneylending, beginning in the 12th century, was to prevent the evil of Christian usury by allowing Jews to engage in that forbidden economic activity.

Remember that in most of Europe in the Middle Ages, Jews were the only tolerated non-Christian minority. They weren't always tolerated, but when they were tolerated, they were the only non-Christian minority. Jews were not subject to the prohibitions of canon law. The notion was that the Jews were condemned in any case to perpetual damnation because of their repudiation of Christ, and so the notion was that the Jews would be allowed to engage in usury.

And so there began an association of moneymaking with the Jews, an association that would further taint attitudes toward commerce among Christians. That's part of the importance of the condemnation of usury and its association with Jews in medieval Christian culture. Usury is not easily distinguished from merchant activity in general. If trade involves buying something with money in order to sell it for more money, how different is that from using money to make more money by lending it out?

A great deal of attention was devoted by the Scholastic theologians to just this problem. What are licit, or legitimate, forms of commerce, and what are illicit forms of commerce that smack of usury, which was unnatural and sinful? Since it was hard for theologians to draw this line, it was even harder for common people to draw the line, and so the condemnation of moneylending as sinful tended to cast a shadow of suspicion over many aspects of merchant activity. Not only that, but the term "usury" came to be applied more broadly to other forms of economic activity that were seen as socially harmful. So usury, then, was a stigmatized category. It was that category of economic activity that was really religiously and morally abhorrent. The religious burden, or the negative connotations, of usury were extended by the fact that this stigmatized activity of usury was attached to this stigmatized minority, that is to say, Jews. That is to say, usury was something that could only be conducted by those who were outside the community of the faithful.

It was not, by the way, that Jews were the only ones who lent out money at interest during the Middle Ages. So did some Christians, including kings and even monasteries, but they weren't supposed to, and the Christians who did lend out money at interest were chastised with the worst insult that Christian theologians could think of, that they were acting like Jews. So lending out money at interest was often described as "Judaizing."

This stigmatization of moneylending through its association with the Jews was important for another reason as well. Namely, you'll recall Aristotle's notion that money was sterile. The truth is that the notion of money as sterile is fundamentally misleading. In that sense, it provides a poor flashlight on certain areas of the world. Money is not sterile if it allows one to buy something earlier than one could otherwise. If you can borrow money and buy a car today rather than having to wait two years, that isn't sterile. It gives you the use of something that you want to buy at an earlier time. Of course, money isn't sterile in a purely monetary sense if you use the money that you borrowed to buy something that you can then sell at a profit.

These productive uses of money didn't occur to Aristotle, and this stigmatization of moneylending as usury, and the notion that usury and the lending of money was sterile, had all sorts of connotations that continued to influence the way in which people thought about money. Because beneath the condemnation of merchants and of moneylending was the very commonly held assumption that only those people whose work produced sweat really worked and really produced. That's something that every peasant or worker in physical activity understands, that he has to work hard—he sweats, he works with his body—he sweats, and therefore he's entitled to something.

In earlier times, many people simply couldn't imagine that production could be increased by products of the mind, by the decision to invest resources in one place rather than another, to buy one thing rather than another, and to buy it at the right time, and to sell it at the right time, to invest money with one person rather than another, in one commodity rather than another. All of this requires gathering information and analyzing information. The economic value of gathering and analyzing information simply was beyond the mental horizon of most of those people who worked on the land or who worked with their hands. The notion of trade, and even more of moneylending, as unproductive was often expressed in images of parasitism. That's the way in which sometimes merchants in general, but often moneylenders in particular, were portrayed: as parasites who somehow sucked the life out of the living, productive, hardworking, physically sweating population.

The priests and those influenced by them tended to regard merchants as moral parasites, and the nobles, whose way of life was based on fighting, tended to regard merchants as unmanly cowards. That, then, was the intellectual backdrop against which European intellectuals came to thinking about capitalism. This set of assumptions and set of images that lingered on for a long time, and often enough in a more attenuated or ghostly form, continues on even into the present.

Lecture Three
Hobbes's Challenge to the Traditions

Scope:

In the 17th century, the Christian and civic republican traditions were subject to fundamental criticism by Thomas Hobbes, especially in his *Leviathan* (1651). Hobbes also pioneered an approach to social analysis based on exploring the passions and the ways they could be put to socially positive uses through institutions. Hobbes's great importance, for our themes, lies in his emphasis on this-worldly happiness as the goal of government; and for his early explorations of the role of self-love in human affairs; and for his abandonment of the notion that the role of government is to guide us to some shared purpose, some highest ideal, be it religious holiness or civic virtue.

Outline

I. In the course of the 17th century, both the civic republican tradition and the Christian tradition came to be challenged.
   A. The religiously based civil wars that tore parts of Europe apart in the 16th and 17th centuries led to a critique of the Christian tradition and a critique of its suspicion of the pursuit of material self-interest.
   B. The thinker who challenged that tradition most incisively was Thomas Hobbes. He probably did more than any other single thinker to bring about the secularization of political thought.
   C. He put forth a way of thinking about human affairs that would be followed by many subsequent thinkers who disagreed with him on one issue or another, such as John Locke.

II. Hobbes not only called into question the Christian ideal of a pious and holy society—he treated it as a danger.
   A. For Hobbes, a key problem was how to rescue people from the fanaticism and strife that religion seemed to bring.
   B. His great book, *Leviathan*, was written in the midst of the English Civil War, or the Puritan Revolution.

- C. Hobbes was a humanist, a person trained in classical and foreign languages who earned his living as the employee of a rich and powerful aristocratic family.
- D. As an advisor to the family, Hobbes became a participant in the leading political controversies and conflicts of the era.

III. Hobbes contended that in thinking about political life, one must not begin with the assumption that man has any intrinsic purpose other than his own survival and worldly well-being.
- A. In point of fact, people don't agree on what their ultimate purposes are, or on how to get there.
- B. Often enough, in the century and a half after the Reformation, they were willing to oppress, expel, or even murder one another to enforce their beliefs.
- C. Hobbes's concern was how to prevent religiously based civil war, and his approach was to try to discover what motivates people.

IV. Hobbes contended that while one couldn't get people to agree on fundamental truths about the purpose of life, one could perhaps get them to agree that everyone wanted to avoid a violent, unexpected death.
- A. Everyone was faced with the constant possibility of a violent death in what Hobbes called "the state of nature" (i.e., any situation in which there is no state capable of enforcing laws equally).
- B. Without a state to enforce such laws, we are all subject to being murdered or deliberately injured for one reason or another.
- C. The one thing that every self-interested person should be able to agree on is the need for an effective government, with a power formidable enough to enforce the rules that make coexistence possible.
- D. That formidable power was what he called "Leviathan," which was another name for the state.

V. Hobbes's vision of the good life is resolutely this-worldly, and the secular world he sought to forge was of individuals living in peace, prosperity, and intellectual development.
   A. The problem for Hobbes was that many people at the time did not value their lives above all: They valued their eternal salvation. Many believed that only by following the claims of their church could they avoid hell and get to heaven.
   B. So Hobbes devoted a good deal of *Leviathan* to questions of religion in general and the Bible in particular.
   C. He tried to deflate religious zeal by pointing out the weak basis for the theological differences over which Christians were willing to kill one another.
   D. He tried to redirect people's concerns from their eternal salvation to their earthly well-being, believing that the prospect of improving their worldly well-being would provide broader grounds for consensus, or at least for peace.

VI. In discussing the passions, Hobbes often evaluated them quite differently from the Christian tradition.
   A. "Covetousness" was regarded by the Catholic tradition as a sin; indeed, it was more or less a synonym for "avarice."
   B. Hobbes defines "covetousness" as the desire for riches and says there is no reason to condemn the desire to get rich as such. It is only when people pursue that desire through illegitimate means that we ought to condemn them.
   C. In Hobbes we see a legitimation of self-interest that would be picked up by many later thinkers.

VII. Hobbes showed that claims to an absolute right of property would undermine the basis of effective property rights.
   A. Among the rights of the sovereign is the collection of taxes.
   B. People are reluctant to pay taxes, Hobbes says, because their self-love makes them short-sighted, so they exaggerate the costs to themselves of paying taxes and fail to see the long-term benefits of having a government that can protect them.
   C. He therefore criticizes the notion that all people have an absolute right to their own property.

D. He argues that without taxation, there is no government, and without effective government, there is no effective private property.

VIII. Hobbes's work was important for the history of thinking about capitalism in a number of ways.
   A. His emphasis on this-worldly happiness as the goal of government advanced the secularization of political thought.
   B. His early explorations of the role of self-interest in human affairs contributed to a trend in early modern thought that was also reflected in French Jansenist Pierre Nicole's "Of Charity and Self-Love" (1675) and in Bernard de Mandeville's *The Fable of the Bees* (1706).
   C. Hobbes's abandonment of the notion that the role of government is to guide us to some shared purpose, some highest ideal—be it religious holiness or civic virtue—set the stage for modern liberalism.
   D. In these respects, he challenged both the Christian tradition and the civic republican tradition.

Suggested Reading:

Hobbes, *Leviathan*.

Oakeshott, *Hobbes on Civil Association*.

Malcolm, *Aspects of Hobbes*, especially the essays "A Summary Biography of Hobbes" and "Hobbes and the European Republic of Letters."

Questions to Consider:

1. Hobbes thought that in order to create a society not driven by religious conflict he had to deflate the confidence of people that their religious denomination offered the only road to salvation. Was he right?
2. Is there a clear distinction between "covetousness" or "greed" or "avarice" and the pursuit of material well-being? Or are the first three terms merely ways of stigmatizing the pursuit of material well-being?

Lecture Three—Transcript
Hobbes's Challenge to the Traditions

In the course of the 17th century, both the civic republican tradition and the Christian tradition came to be challenged. In this lecture and the next, we'll see how that came about. In the next lecture, we'll look at how the economic and political transformations of the Netherlands led to a reconsideration and reformulation of the civic republican tradition.

In this lecture, I want to look at the intellectual changes that came about in reaction against the religiously based civil wars that tore parts of Europe apart in the 16th and 17th centuries. That reaction led to a critique of the Christian tradition and a critique of its suspicion of the pursuit of material self-interest.

The thinker who challenged that tradition most openly, most explicitly, and most incisively was Thomas Hobbes. He probably did more than any other single thinker to bring about the secularization of political thought. He put forth a way of thinking about human affairs that would be followed by many subsequent thinkers, even those who disagreed with him on one issue or another, such as John Locke.

The Christian and civic republican traditions were both normative traditions. By that I mean they were conceptions of what ideally ought to be the case. When we say that the civic republican ideal dominated in ancient Greece, or that it was revived in Renaissance Italy, we don't mean that most people actually acted according to the values of selfless citizenship and devotion to the city-state, but that was the cultural ideal articulated by the great thinkers of the age. Similarly, when we say that the Christian tradition was culturally dominant during the Middle Ages and well into the 17th century, we don't mean that everyone lived up to Christian ideals, or even that most people did. We mean that the cultural spokesmen of the time, who were mostly clerics, held out the ideal of a holy and pious society, of a society leading to salvation as the desirable standard by which to measure their societies.

Thomas Hobbes not only called the Christian ideal into question, he treated it as a danger. For Hobbes, the problem was not what was the correct religious approach to commerce or to any other problem. For Hobbes, religion *was* the problem. He was living in an era marked by religious war, often in the form of civil wars between religious factions. And so for Hobbes a key problem was how to rescue people from what he saw as the fanaticism and strife that religion seemed to bring with it. In other words, Hobbes saw religion primarily as a source of conflict, which in his own day was leading to civil war.

His great book, *Leviathan*, was written in the midst of the English Civil War, or the Puritan Revolution, which pitted the king and the Church of England on the one hand against the Parliament dominated by Calvinists, or Puritans and Presbyterians, as they were known in Great Britain. At that very time central Europe was being wracked by the Thirty Years' War, which pitted Catholics, Lutherans, and Calvinists against one another in a series of conflicts that led to the death of more than 30 percent of the population of German-speaking Europe.

Who was Thomas Hobbes? He was the son of a country clergyman of the Church of England. His father was ill-educated, badly compensated, but then he seems to have spent more time in the ale house than in the pulpit. But young Thomas was different. He was sent to Oxford University, possibly to become a curate like his father, since a career in the church was considered a safe way to earn a living. But young Thomas was obviously brilliant, and he was trained as a humanist, that is to say, a person trained in classical and foreign languages. But what did a person trained in classical and foreign languages do for a living? Well, Hobbes earned his living, as did most humanists, and that was as the employee of a rich and powerful aristocratic family. In other words, under the system that we call "patronage." In Hobbes's case, he was an employee of the Cavendish family, where he served as a tutor, secretary, and sort of all-around advisor. Part of that role was to accompany the teenage sons of the family on the grand tour of continental Europe, to Italy and to France, which brought Hobbes into contact with leading scientists and philosophers in Italy and France, including Galileo.

As an advisor to the family, Hobbes became a participant in the leading political controversies and conflicts of his era. The Earl of Cavendish was a member of Parliament, and he also sat on the board of the newly founded Virginia Company. Hobbes attended the meetings of the Virginia Company's governing board, and there he came into contact with many prominent politicians of the day.

Hobbes had a remarkable range of interests. He translated Thucydides into English. He wrote about optics and about other scientific subjects, but the increasing political conflicts of the 1630s and 1640s drew his attention evermore to politics.

In 1640, there was a dispute between the king and the dominant faction in Parliament, which was opposed to the king on religious grounds, among others, over the king's power. Hobbes, at that point, published a tract in favor of royal power. In the years thereafter, as the antiroyal forces grew in power, Hobbes feared for his life and for his safety, and so he fled to Paris. There, he promptly found himself in the midst of another civil war, the Fronde, as it's known, which also had a religious dimension to it. It was there, in Paris in 1649–1650, that Hobbes wrote *Leviathan*, which many people consider to be the greatest work of philosophy written in English.

The book was intended to have immediate relevance to civil wars going on both in England and in France. In fact, as Hobbes was there in Paris writing the book in English chapter by chapter, it was being translated into French because it was supposed to have relevance for the French civil war as well. So this work that was written for a particular occasion also had ongoing perennial interests.

Hobbes contends that in thinking about politics we have to lay out our premises and build upon them. We shouldn't begin with an idealized view of how man ought to be. We shouldn't assume, in thinking about politics, that man has any intrinsic purpose other than his own survival and his worldly well-being. We can't assume, in other words, that we know what man's purpose is, that man's purpose is to be holy or pious, or to be a citizen, and the way to get to salvation is through x, y, and z. We can't assume that we know what man's purpose is because in point of fact men don't agree on what their ultimate purposes are, and they don't agree on how to get there. *That* Hobbes could see all around him.

Some believe that the ultimate purpose of life is salvation leading to eternal life in heaven. Many people at the time thought that, but they disagreed about how to get to heaven. Most thought that the only way to get to heaven was through their church. It was a key belief of Roman Catholicism, for example, that outside the church there is no salvation. But after the Protestant Reformation, which occurred in the second quarter of the 16th century, Lutherans, Anglicans, Calvinists, and many smaller Christian groups all believed the same thing. They all believed that only their church led to salvation. They disagreed about which church would bring salvation, which church rites, which rituals, which dogmas, which clergymen. Often enough, in the century and a half after the Reformation, they were willing to oppress one another, expel one another, or even murder one another to enforce their beliefs, and they were willing to go to war for their beliefs.

Hobbes's concern, then, his overriding concern was how to prevent religiously based civil war. His approach was to try to discover, as he put it, "how men really are." That means discovering what motivates them. What motivates them, Hobbes says, is in good part their passions, or what we would now call their emotions, and also to some degree their reason, which is linked to their passions. Therefore, Hobbes says, one has to look at human psychology, which is the subject of the first part of *Leviathan*.

Hobbes contended that one couldn't get men to agree by reason or by faith on fundamental truths about the purpose of life or about ultimate salvation. But although one might not be able to get people to agree on a conception of the best society, it might be possible to get them to agree rationally on institutional arrangements that would guarantee a bare minimum of earthly happiness. If you couldn't get them to agree on what was the best for a society and government, you could perhaps get them to agree on what was the worst: What was the situation that everyone wanted to avoid? And so Hobbes asks, what is it that every person fears? His answer is "death," or more exactly, a violent, unexpected death. Hobbes argued that everyone was faced with the constant possibility of a violent death in what Hobbes calls "the state of nature," or what we might call "the law of the jungle." "The state of nature" referred to any situation in which there is no state capable of enforcing laws equally; that is to say, it may refer to some earlier period of history, but it is a recurrent phenomenon whenever the state is not strong enough to enforce the rule of law. In that sense, Hobbes thought that much of Europe at the time was in a state of nature. Whenever you're in a neighborhood where you can't depend on the law for your life or your property, Hobbes would say you're back in the state of nature.

The first law that needed to be enforced was "thou shalt not murder." You might think that's a universal law, but without a state to enforce such laws, we're all subject to being murdered or deliberately injured by some individual or some group that wants to kill us for one reason or another, perhaps because they want our property, or perhaps because we offend their pride. We dis them in one way or another.

The state of nature also exists in any circumstance, then, where individuals can't rely upon government to protect their lives, to prevent violent death. That's especially the case in civil war, when half the population is trying to kill the other half. Hobbes's contention was that the proper role of government was not to create a holy society, since men didn't agree on what was holy, and in that sense he was a critic of the Christian ideal.

He was also a critic of the civic republican ideal, the notion that citizens had a necessary right and responsibility to participate in governing. It's not that he thought that participating in government was bad, but he thought that it was much less important than having an effective government, a government that can keep the peace. He said, What use is it to have a situation where you can participate in government if the government is so split, or it's so ineffective, that it can't protect your life?

The one thing that every self-interested person should be able to agree on, Hobbes argued, was the need for an effective government, a government strong enough to do whatever was needed to protect against foreign invaders and against internal civil war. If people came to that rational agreement, Hobbes argued, they would be able to form a commonwealth with a power formidable enough to enforce the rules that made coexistence possible between people who would otherwise be a threat to one another. That formidable power was what Hobbes called "Leviathan," which was another name for the state.

In place of the religious life of the pious, or the political life of those who govern and fight, Hobbes laid out an alternate vision of the good life with his own set of virtues. Instead of religious otherworldliness, Hobbes's vision is resolutely this-worldly, and the secular world that he tried to forge was one of individuals living in peace, in prosperity, and in intellectual development.

The problem for Hobbes was that many people at the time didn't value their lives above all. They valued their eternal salvation. They thought that this life was short and fleeting. Eternal salvation or eternal damnation went on forever, and many believed that only by following the claims of their church could they avoid hell and get to heaven. That's why Hobbes devoted so much of *Leviathan* to questions of religion in general and interpreting the Bible in particular. He tried to deflate religious zeal by pointing out the weak basis for the theological differences over which Christians were willing to kill one another. He showed that the Bible was far less clear than most believers supposed, and that its political claims were far more limited and far less relevant than most believers in the 17th century imagined. He tried to demonstrate that salvation didn't depend on the theological differences that divided Catholics from Protestants, or Protestants from one another, or even Christians from Jews. He tried to redirect men's concerns from their eternal salvation to their earthly well-being, believing that the prospect of improving their worldly well-being would provide a broader basis for consensus, or at least for peace.

As you might imagine, Hobbes's arguments aroused tremendous opposition in his day from Christians of various sorts: from Catholics, from Anglicans, from Puritans, from Presbyterians, from Lutherans, and so on, but his arguments were tremendously influential in the late 17th century and afterwards, influential first in their focus on this-worldly well-being and the notion that political claims and religious claims ought to be divorced from one another.

Hobbes was influential in another way as well, and that was in his insistence that in thinking about social and political institutions, one had to begin by seeing men as they are, rather than beginning with how we'd like them to be. That meant paying attention to the passions, to human psychology. In discussing the passions, Hobbes often evaluated them quite differently from the way in which they had been evaluated in the Christian tradition.

Take, for example, covetousness, which was regarded by the Catholic tradition as a sin; indeed, it was more or less a synonym for avarice. In the early part of *Leviathan*, Hobbes defines "covetousness" as the desire for riches. He says that people usually use the term "covetousness" as a term of disapproval. We don't call people covetous whose actions we approve of. But people use the term with these negative connotations, Hobbes says, because people compete with one another for riches, and the ones who do less well are displeased with the ones who do more well. In other words, he suggests to refer to those who do better, who get rich, as covetousness is really a cover for human envy. Actually, he says, there is no reason to condemn the desire to get rich, as such. It's only when men pursue that desire through illegitimate means that we ought to condemn them. So in Hobbes, we have a legitimation of self-interest, including material self-interest, that would be picked up by many later thinkers up to the present day.

Hobbes doesn't say much directly about economic matters in *Leviathan*, but what he does say is of interest. When he comes to discuss the rights of the sovereign, and the sovereign for Hobbes can be a monarch, or it can be a representative Parliament. In other words, when he comes to discuss the rights of government, he says that one of those rights is the right to collect taxes. Hobbes says, and this may sound familiar, that people always grumble about government. They grumble about government whether the sovereign is a monarch or an elected government. They forget that every form of government has some faults and certain disadvantages, but they forget that almost any form of functioning government is preferable to a situation without functioning government, which leaves men unrestrained in their desires to rob and murder one another. So they underrate what they are getting out of government.

They also forget that in order to defend themselves from foreign enemies, the citizens of a state need a government that is capable of defending them, and that in order to defend them it needs to raise revenue, and to do that it needs taxes. But people are reluctant to pay their taxes, Hobbes says, and they're reluctant to pay their taxes because their self-love makes them shortsighted, so they exaggerate the costs to themselves of paying taxes, and they fail to see the long-term benefits of having a government that can protect them.

Another economically related notion that Hobbes criticizes as a source of potential civil war and a source of the dissolution of government is the notion that everyone has an absolute right to his own property. Now, Hobbes is not against private property. He thinks that it's very important to have a situation where no individual is allowed to take the property of another individual. But without a government to protect us and to enforce the laws, every individual has to fear that other individuals will seize his property. So the government, in order to be able to provide that protection, does have to have a right to some of your property, Hobbes says, in the form of taxation. Otherwise, without taxation, there's no government, and with no government, there is no effective private property.

Part of Hobbes's great importance, then, for the history of thinking about capitalism comes from his early explorations of the role of the passions, especially the passions of self-love and self-interest, and his more positive evaluation of the role of self-interest.

That theme of the potential positive uses of self-love and self-interest was also being discovered elsewhere in 17th-century Europe. Some of the people who did the most to contribute to that reevaluation were the Jansenists. The Jansenists were a group of Catholic theologians who returned to St. Augustine's notion of man's "fallenness" because of his depravity, of the notion that without God's grace, men cannot really act charitably toward one another or benevolently toward one another, as we would see. And the Jansenists began as moral rigorists; that is to say, they were constantly exploring human behavior to see what they regarded as the sin of pride, which was related to self-love—what role pride and self-love played in human behavior.

As they explored human actions through this set of concepts, they found that a great deal of what appeared to be virtuous or charitable action was actually due to pride and self-love—above all, people's desire for the approval of others. That's related to pride, and the Jansenists concluded that many people engaged in actions that seemed to be charitable and benevolent, but it couldn't really be a product of true charity because true charity was based on God's grace, and these people couldn't have God's grace because they weren't Catholics. So how is it that non-Catholics, the people who clearly didn't have God's grace, were able to act in ways that seemed to be, that were apparently, virtuous and benevolent? The Jansenists traced this to pride and self-love.

Here's a quote from one of their great theorists, the Frenchman Pierre Nicole, who in the late 17th century published an essay on charity and self-love. He says, "Although nothing is more opposed to charity which relates everything to God than self-love which revolves entirely around the self, yet there is nothing more similar to the effects of charity than [those of] self-love."

In other words, people, because of a desire for the approval of others, often act in ways that appear to be virtuous and benevolent. Nicole goes on to say that behind commerce lies a sin, the sin of cupidity, but he says that it's through commerce that all the needs of society are in some fashion fulfilled without charity playing any role whatsoever. And he says that as a result, in states where true religion has been banished—that is to say, states that are non-Catholic—one lives in no less peace, security, and comfort than if one were in a republic of saints.

So here you see the beginning of this rediscovery on the Continent of the positive uses of self-love. It was left for other thinkers to drop Nicole's theological premises about man's absolute fallenness and to say, all right, you've showed us that there are positive uses of self-love and self-interest. Let's explore that theme.

One of the ones who explored it in a way that was regarded as scandalous at the time, but was highly influential, was a Dutch physician by the name of Bernard de Mandeville, who in the late 17th century moved to England and became a well-known publicist. In 1706, he published a poem called *The Fable of the Bees*, together with a long commentary on the poem. In *The Fable of the Bees*, the bees who had lived in an industrious, productive, comfortable situation based on all of these vices—based on self-love, based on their pursuit of self-interest, based on vanity—they give up all these character traits that had traditionally been stigmatized as sins. When they give them up, they end up living in a society that is unproductive, barren, quiet, and boring.

This was a way of bringing out to a larger public this reevaluation of the role of self-love and self-interest that was going on in late 17th-and early 18th-century Europe. This is a theme that we will see explored when we turn to Voltaire and to Adam Smith.

So part of Hobbes's significance, then, is in his exploration of the passions and his upward evaluation, you might say, of the role of self-love. His greatest significance, perhaps, is for his emphasis on this-worldly happiness as the goal of government, and above all for his abandonment of the notion that the role of government is to guide us, collectively, to some shared purpose, some highest ideal—be it the religious ideal of holiness and salvation or some civic republican ideal. In all of these respects, Hobbes challenged both the Christian tradition and the civic republican tradition. He set the stage for the work of John Locke and for what became known as liberalism, that is, the notion that the role of the state is to protect us from foreign and internal violence—but that the state should allow us, as individuals, to pursue the goals that we deem to be highest, to devote ourselves (to use a slightly later formulation) to the pursuit of happiness.

The pursuit of happiness; that was a radical idea when it was put forward in the 17th century. If nowadays we take it for granted, if it has come to permeate our thought, we owe that in no small part to Thomas Hobbes.

Lecture Four
Dutch Commerce and National Power

Scope:

In the 17th century, the Dutch Republic provided an example of a highly commercial society with increasing national power. The Dutch East India Company, which transported luxury goods from what are now India and Indonesia to Europe, became the most important commercial enterprise in the world. To conduct their overseas trade, the Dutch developed into a major naval power. Thus commerce and national power were interlinked, leading European thinkers to reformulate the civic republican tradition in a more commercial direction.

Outline

I. In the course of the 17th century, the civic republican tradition was transformed with the growing recognition that trade and commerce were essential elements of national power and political survival.
   - A. The increase of material wealth came to be seen as part of the logic of state power.
   - B. This close interweaving between political power and economic policy became "political economy," a term first used, in French, in 1615.
   - C. It also led to two divergent ways to achieve national power: through free trade and through the policy of protecting national commerce against foreign competition.

II. When 17th- and 18th-century European thinkers considered issues of national power, they inevitably had to think about the United Provinces of the Netherlands.
   - A. Though it was a small country without significant natural resources, it was rich, and powerful enough militarily to fend off attacks by nations that were far larger in population and natural resources.
   - B. Because the Dutch were the most commercially oriented nation in Europe, their success raised the issue of the links between commerce and national power.

C. By the late 16th century, the Dutch became the dominant power in world commerce, a position that they maintained for almost a century and a half.

III. How did they do it?
A. For much of the 16th century, the Netherlands, together with what is now Belgium, had been part of the Spanish empire, until they revolted and attained their independence.
B. The Dutch profited from the influx of Calvinist refugees from Antwerp, which had been the center of European commerce—refugees who brought with them capital and skills in artisanal trades.
C. Holland was also a magnet for the Marranos, or crypto-Jews—a prime example of a diasporic merchant minority—who brought with them their capital and commercial contacts in Spain, Portugal, and the Spanish empire.
D. Holland thus profited by becoming a center of religious toleration.

IV. The Dutch moved into intercontinental trade and then into colonization.
A. Prohibited from trade with the Spanish and Portuguese empires, Dutch merchants decided that they had to go to the sources of the "rich trades."
B. To do so, the Dutch pioneered the creation of merchant companies to pool capital and risk for large-scale single undertakings.
C. In 1602, they formed the Dutch East India Company, the first multinational corporation and the first company to issue stock.
D. Dividing ownership in this way meant that people with smaller amounts of money could come to own part of the company.

V. To trade in the East Indies, the Dutch developed a powerful navy, which they used to spread their commercial reach.
A. The Dutch East India Company set up trading posts in the Spice Islands and Indonesia and drove out the British and the Portuguese by armed might.

- B. The company established a colony on the Cape of Good Hope and outposts across much of coastal Asia, in what are now Iran, India, and Malaysia.
- C. The government of the United Provinces had granted the company the right to make treaties and engage in war on behalf of the United Provinces.
- D. By 1669, the East India Company was the richest private company the world had ever seen.

VI. By the mid-17th century, the Dutch were clearly the most commercially oriented nation in Europe.
- A. To make it easier to find funds for new ventures, they created stock markets, at which shares of the East India Company and other companies could be bought and sold.
- B. The United Provinces were also the center of international finance, and the Bank of Amsterdam, founded in 1609, was the most important bank in Europe.
- C. They developed a number of industries as well. These were essentially artisanal, but with a substantial division of labor.
- D. Many of these industries involved new commodities that began as luxuries oriented to the rich but were becoming accessible to a much wider population.
- E. Holland was perhaps the first society in which a majority of households made the switch in allocation of time toward production for the market.

VII. Dutch politicians and political publicists began writing books on the links between the preservation of the republic and its commercial strength.
- A. The best known of these was *The True Interest and Political Maxims of the Republic of Holland*, published in 1662 by Pieter de la Court. He argued that the power of Holland to defend itself depended upon free trade policies.
- B. Nicholas Barbon, an English author, wrote in his *Discourse of Trade* in 1690 that the problem with political thinkers was that they had said almost nothing about trade and its importance to the state.

C. By the early 18th century, we increasingly find political thinkers writing about commerce as part of politics, giving rise to "political economy."

VIII. De la Court's views on freedom of trade were very much a minority position. Most political writers and politicians in Britain and France were more inclined to government policies that later came to be called "mercantilism." They sought to take commerce away from the Dutch.

   A. The implicit assumption of mercantilist policies was that international wealth was fixed, so international economic relations were a zero-sum game, in which gains for one nation could only come at the expense of other nations.
   B. The result of this way of thinking was war and protectionism.
   C. To try to strengthen their own cause and weaken that of the Dutch, Britain, France, and other European countries developed protectionist policies that made it difficult or impossible for the Dutch to control international trade.
   D. By 1720, the Dutch no longer dominated international commerce.
   E. What had happened in 17th-century Holland set the stage for a series of debates in the 18th century and beyond.

Suggested Reading:

Clark, *Commerce, Culture and Liberty* (the selections from Pieter de la Court's *Political Maxims of the State of Holland* and Nicholas Barbon's *A Discourse of Trade*).

Viner, *Essays on the Intellectual History of Economics*, especially the essays "Power versus Plenty as Objectives of Foreign Policy in the Seventeenth and Eighteenth Centuries" and "Mercantilist Thought."

Hont, *Jealousy of Trade*, "Free Trade and the Economic Limits to National Politics."

Questions to Consider:

1. To what degree is military power a prerequisite for a nation's economic growth?
2. How does economic stagnation or growth affect a nation's military power?

Lecture Four—Transcript
Dutch Commerce and National Power

While Hobbes, in his great book *Leviathan*, had called the Christian ideal into question in response to the age of religious wars, the civic republican tradition began to undergo a sort of internal transformation as well, also in response to new historical developments. You recall that the civic republican tradition, going back to those ancient Greek city-states, had emphasized the nobility of self-sacrifice on behalf of the city-state, the importance of military service in defense of the state, and the importance of participating in government. That had gone together, you'll recall, with a suspicion of those who were engaged in commerce and a suspicion of wealth. The fear was that the pursuit of wealth could lead to corruption, a situation where citizens put their private material interests above those of the commonwealth and its defense.

In the course of the 17th century, the civic republican tradition was not so much abandoned as transformed, or to put it in another way, it was commercialized, as there was a growing recognition that trade and commerce was an essential element of national power and, hence, of political survival. The increase in material wealth came to be seen as part of the logic of state power because the state needed material means in order to be able to conduct war against other states, or in order to defend itself militarily against attacks from those other states. This close interweaving between political power and economic policy gave birth to a new genre of writing that came to be called "political economy," a term that was first used in French in 1615.

It also led to two divergent recipes for achieving national power. One formula led toward a policy of free trade, and the second formula led toward a policy of trying to protect national commerce against foreign competition.

When 17th- and 18th-century European thinkers considered issues of national power, they inevitably had to think about Holland, or as it was properly called, the United Provinces of the Netherlands. Here was a country without many natural resources. It didn't have gold or silver, for example. It was a country that was small in population, about 2 million compared to 6 million in Great Britain, but it was a country that was rich. Historians estimate that in 1700, the per capita GNP, that is, the amount of wealth per person in Holland, was about

50 percent higher than in Great Britain, which itself was a relatively well-to-do country at the time.

This Dutch state was powerful enough militarily to fend off attacks by nations that were far larger in population and in natural resources. And at a time when most countries in Europe were ruled as monarchies, the Dutch were a republic. Looking at Holland from elsewhere in Europe, one couldn't help being struck by the fact that these rich and powerful Dutchmen had become powerful through trade, because Holland in the 17th century was the most commercially-oriented nation in Europe.

Since the 16th century, the Dutch had built themselves into a remarkable commercial power. At first, with few natural resources, they became a seagoing and trading people. At first they imported primary goods from Scandinavia and from eastern Europe, products like grain or timber or hides, and they exported those to western and southern Europe. These were items that were low-value items, where profit was to be made by transporting them in bulk, by selling a lot of them. The Dutch also exported fish from the sea—above all, herring, which they exported to the rest of Europe. You could say that the Dutch success was built on the back of the herring.

Fish was an important source of protein for most Europeans in the 17th century, and for much of the year in many parts of Europe, fish was available only in salted form. From about 1500 on, the Dutch came to dominate the European herring market, and they did so by a remarkable act of ingenuity: the factory ship. This was a ship that was capable of going out into the ocean. It had a deep hull, a crew of up to 30 people, and these could go out into the Atlantic Ocean, really as far as the American coast. That meant a voyage of five, six, seven, even eight weeks at a time.

The question was, how do you keep fish edible for eight weeks at a time, indeed, edible enough that one can then export them elsewhere in Europe? The Dutch developed a system where they followed the herring into the sea, they caught them in large nets, and then they gutted them and salted them within a matter of hours on the ship itself so that the fish could be preserved for weeks and even months.

By the 16th century, the Dutch had a fleet of 400 or 500 of these oceangoing ships. So it began with herring, and then in the last decades of the 16th century and the first decades of the 17th, the

Dutch expanded into what were called the "rich trades," that is to say, trades in high-value products from distant parts of the world. Some of these were traditional luxury products, products that were very expensive, highly valuable, such as cinnamon, or nutmeg, or Chinese porcelain. Others were new products that were being imported from Asia and from the Americas, products for which Europeans were developing a taste. What were these new products? Tea, coffee, sugar, tobacco. You'll notice that these were all products with pharmacological properties.

At first, these new products were luxury products in the 17th century, but in the course of the 18th century, they were increasingly coming to be regarded as necessities, as something that everybody needed, and well down into the social ladder. Some of these products, especially sugar and tobacco, were produced in the New World, using slave labor of enslaved Africans, and the Dutch were involved in the trade in slaves as well.

From the late 16th century, then, the Dutch became the dominant power in world commerce, a position that they maintained through about 1720, that is to say, for almost a century and a half. How did they do it? For much of the 16th century, the Netherlands, together with what is now Belgium, had been part of the Spanish empire. In the middle of the 16th century, during the Protestant Reformation, substantial parts of the population of the Netherlands and of Belgium converted to Calvinism. Philip II, the most Catholic emperor of Spain, relied on the Inquisition to try to restore Catholic orthodoxy in the Netherlands, and that led them into revolt. In the end, the northern provinces, what we now think of as the Netherlands (or Holland), attained their independence, while the southern provinces, what we now call Belgium, remained part of Philip's empire. This was very important in terms of changes in world trade because the main city of those southern provinces was Antwerp, which in the 17th century had been the center of European commerce.

Antwerp had a large Calvinist population, and now, with the success of the revolt of the northern provinces, these people, about 38,000 of them—which was about half the population of Antwerp—now moved north to the Netherlands, especially to Amsterdam and Rotterdam. They brought with them their capital, and also skills in artisanal trades like weaving.

Holland was also a magnet for another sort of refugees, people who were variously called Marranos or crypto-Jews or New Christians or Jews. These were people whose ancestors had been Jews in Spain. They had prospered there in the medieval period. They had prospered as merchants. They had also been active as moneylenders, including to the king and to nobles, and the king also used them to collect his taxes. None of this made them particularly popular, and there was increasing pressure on them, riots against them, massacres against them in 1390, and Jews were given the choice of converting to Catholicism or being massacred. Some of them did convert to Catholicism, and then they were given the name "New Christians." As New Christians, as people who were no longer bound by the rules that limited Jewish occupations, they tended to thrive, and that in turn caused new antagonism against them, plus there was a few that the New Christians were interacting and were returning back to Judaism because of the influence of the existing Jews.

All of this led to a situation where in 1492, the Jews were expelled from Spain. Some of them went to Portugal, where they were expelled a few years later, and then some of them went to the Ottoman Empire, especially to Salonica. Some of them, in an attempt to escape the Inquisition, went to Spanish colonies like Curacao, Portuguese colonies like Brazil. A substantial number of these crypto-Jews—that is to say, people who were outwardly Christian but who wanted to practice Judaism and did so in secret—came to northern Europe hoping to be able to practice their Judaism openly. Some came to Antwerp, and then when Antwerp was separated from the Netherlands, they made their way to Amsterdam, where many of them returned to Judaism.

This group of people, some of whom were Christians, some of whom were crypto-Jews, some of whom were actual Jews, these people formed a very interesting example of a phenomenon that we find frequently in the history of the development of capitalism, and that is of diasporic merchant minorities. Diasporic; that is to say, they were in the Diaspora. They were outside of their country of origin. In this case, their country of origin was the land of Israel, where the Jews had lost political sovereignty in A.D. 70.

They were a minority in the countries in which they lived. They were quite oriented towards merchant activity, and in this particular circumstance in early modern Europe, this group of Jews played a particularly important role in linking up commerce in the various parts of Europe and, really, the various parts of the world, because when they came from Spain and Portugal to Antwerp and then to Amsterdam, they brought with them their capital, and more importantly, they brought with them commercial contacts. One of the hardest things to know when you're engaged in international trade is who is there to trade with? Who is there who knows somewhere in some port far away how to get the commodity that you want to import?

Then there is the question of trust. If you're a merchant in Amsterdam and you're selling something, or you're buying (more likely in this case), you're buying something from a merchant in Portugal, how are you going to know that he's going to deliver, and how is he going to know that you're going to pay him? And so the issue of trust becomes very important in international trade. One of the advantages that this diasporic merchant minority had was the fact that they had a common language—they mostly spoke Spanish—and they were often related to one another, or at least knew one another. That means that their communities in each country were able to enforce a certain social discipline. If some merchant in that community was known to be untrustworthy, word would get around, and he would be chastised.

Last, but not least, the advantage that this diasporic minority had was their access to news and information about where goods were to be had, what was the situation of ships on the sea, and so on. So in all of those ways, they played an important role in linking up trade across the Atlantic, in trade between north and southern Europe, and even trade between Europe and the Ottoman Empire.

Holland also profited by becoming a center of religious toleration. It had brought these Calvinists from Antwerp, it had brought these crypto-Jews and Jews from southern Europe, and all of them had contributed to its commercial advance.

The Dutch moved into intercontinental trade and from intercontinental trade to actual colonization, because of the force of necessity. By 1598, the king of Spain, who was then the king of Portugal as well, was alarmed by the growing power of his former Dutch subjects, and in 1598, Dutch trade with Portugal was prohibited. That meant that Dutch merchants and Dutch ships couldn't conduct business in Portugal.

Until then, Dutch merchants had sent ships to Portugal, where they purchased goods from the Portuguese Empire, some of which was located in the New World, in Brazil, some of which was located in South Asia, and they transported these goods from Portugal and sold them across northern Europe.

Now, thanks to this prohibition by the king of Spain and Portugal, that trade was cut off. So the Dutch merchants decided that they had to go to the sources of the rich trades, that is to say, those trades in spices, in silks, and in sugar. But to do that they needed huge resources, more than any individual merchant would have the wherewithal to mobilize. And so the Dutch pioneered the creation of merchant companies to conduct international commerce. At first, the Dutch merchants created companies to pool their capital and risk for one single, large-scale undertaking—for example, to outfit a set of ships that would sail around the Cape of Africa and across the Indian Ocean to what was called the Spice Islands, what we now call the Moluccas that are part of Indonesia.

The Spice Islands play such a big role in this story because they were the only place in the world where nutmeg and cloves were grown, and these were very valuable luxury spices. So the companies were originally set up to fund a single voyage, and then when the ships came home the companies were liquidated.

As competition between these companies intensified, the price of these rich goods went down, and that threatened the profitability of the trade. So the Dutch government decided to try to promote the national interest by creating one company that would have a monopoly on the right to trade in spices. They formed, in 1602, the Dutch East India Company, which was probably the first multinational corporation, and it was the first company to issue stock, that is to say, shares in the company that could be bought and sold. By dividing ownership this way, it meant that people with smaller amounts of money, people who didn't have the means to fund a whole voyage on their own, could come to own part of the company.

The problem for the Dutch East India Company was that other European powers had gotten to the East Indies first, especially the Portuguese, who wanted to maintain their own monopoly on this very valuable trade in spices. So in order to be able to trade in East India, the Dutch had to battle the Portuguese, as well as some local rulers. They had to battle the British, who had set up their own East India company, and that made them competitors against the Dutch, and soon enough the French set up their own East India company as well. All of these companies, then, were in competition, including military competition.

So the Dutch developed a powerful navy in order to be able to pursue international trade. The Dutch East India Company was a remarkable organization. It set up trading posts in the Spice Islands in what we now call Indonesia, and in the decades that followed, they drove out the British and the Portuguese by armed might. The company traded throughout Asia. Ships sailed from Holland to Indonesia. They were sometimes carrying silver from Spanish mines in Peru and supplies for the company's outposts. The silver was used to buy textiles and silk and ceramics in India and China, and then those goods were either sold elsewhere in Asia in order to buy the spices, or some of them were brought back to Europe to be sold there.

The Dutch established a colony on the Cape of Good Hope, that is to say, the southernmost point of Africa, and they established outposts across much of coastal Asia in what is now Iran, India, and Malaysia. So this was no ordinary company.

The government of the United Provinces had granted the company the right to make treaties and engage in war on behalf of the United Provinces. In short, the company was a sort of floating state engaged not only in trade, but in war—and eventually rule over its colonies.

By 1669, the Dutch East India Company was the richest private company the world had ever seen, with over 150 merchant ships, 40 warships, 50,000 employees, a private army of 10,000 soldiers, and a dividend payment of 40 percent. So by the mid-17th century, the Dutch were clearly the most commercially oriented nation in Europe. They dominated world trade, and to make it easier to fund new ventures, they created a stock market at which shares of the East India Company and other such companies could be bought and sold.

The United Provinces was also the center of international finance. The Bank of Amsterdam was founded in 1609, and it was the most important bank in Europe, not so much because it lent out money, but because it was a place where merchants from many countries would have accounts, which made it easy to transfer money to one another.

But Holland wasn't just a trading state. By the mid-17th century, it had developed a number of industries as well. Some of these industries were connected to its maritime strength, industries like shipbuilding or sail making. Other industries were based on processing goods that were brought in from the New World, like sugar refining or tobacco spinning. And then there were industries in the area of textiles: a woolen industry, a silk industry, a cotton industry. One of the most important industries was the whale oil industry, from which the Dutch made oil for lamps. And then there was delftware, which was a variety of pottery that began as an imitation of Chinese porcelain. Chinese porcelain was one of those high-value, high-cost luxury products that had been imported into Holland by the East India Company.

In 1620, when the supply was cut off from China temporarily, Dutch potters decided to try to make their own imitations—imitations that were much cheaper and so could be sold to a much wider market. These industries were essentially artisanal; that is to say, they weren't mechanized. The goods were made by hand, not by machine. But some of them, especially in the textile industries, were made with a substantial division of labor, that is to say, by breaking up the work process—a system that we'll examine when we come to Adam Smith.

What many of these goods had in common was that they represented new commodities that began as luxuries oriented to the rich but that were now becoming accessible to a much wider population, who could afford to buy a wider range of clothes thanks to this textile industry; who could eat better, thanks to the herring trade; who could eat in greater comfort, thanks to dishes from Delft; who could see better at night, thanks to improved lamp oil from the whale oil; and who could now get a buzz from tobacco, tea, coffee, and sugar.

Holland, then, was the wealthiest and most urbanized region of Europe. It seemed to overflow with food and drink and tobacco. One shining example of that wealth came in 1669. It was then that Amsterdam gained the first public street lighting system.

Holland was perhaps the first society in which a majority of households made that switch in the allocation of time toward production for the market. Whether as merchants, as artisans, as wage laborers working in the manufactories of Delft, or wage labor in the form of cottage industry, more and more people were orienting more and more of their time to market-oriented work, and they were doing so because there were more and more goods that they could buy as a result.

So for people who thought about politics and what we would now call "public policy," the Dutch experience was one that seemed to call out for attention. Dutch politicians and political publicists began writing books on the links between the preservation of the republic and its commercial strength.

One of the most famous was Pieter de la Court, a textile manufacturer from Leiden who became a political publicist and in 1662 published a book that got a lot of attention, both in Holland and elsewhere, a book called *The True Interest and Political Maxims of the Republic of Holland*. There he linked republican themes to free trade by arguing that the power of Holland to defend itself depended upon free trade policies.

Here are some of its maxims: "Freedom for all people that will cohabit with us, to follow any occupation for a livelihood." So, freedom of occupation. "That monopolizing companies and guilds which exclude all other persons from their societies, are very prejudicial to Holland." So again, freedom of trade, freedom of occupation.

Here was another one of his maxims: "That toleration regarding the worship of God is a powerful means to preserve many inhabitants in Holland, and attract foreigners to dwell among us." So, the theme of the link between trade and toleration.

Nicholas Barbon, an English author, wrote in his *Discourse of Trade* in 1690 that the problem with political thinkers heretofore, from the ancients through Machiavelli, was that they had said almost nothing about trade and its importance to the state. As that consciousness set in in Britain, the British translated de la Court's book on *The True Interest and Political Maxims of Holland*.

So by the early 18th century, we increasingly find thinkers about politics writing about commerce as part of politics, giving rise to what came to be called "political economy." But de la Court's views on freedom of trade were very much a minority position, this advocacy of free trade as the road to national wealth and national power.

Most political writers and most politicians in Britain and France were more inclined to government policies that came to be called "mercantilism." They looked at the thriving Dutch commercial republic and they asked, how can we take commerce away from the Dutch and get it for ourselves? Now, implicit in this was a psychology of limited wealth, the assumption that international wealth was fixed so that international relations were what we would now call a "zero-sum game," in which gains for one nation could only come at the expense of other nations. The result of this way of thinking was war and protectionism, and so in the 17th and 18th centuries we have a never-ending series of, essentially, wars to control trade among the Spanish and the Dutch and the English and the French.

In order to try to strengthen their own cause and weaken that of the Dutch, Britain, and France, other European countries developed protectionist policies that made it more difficult or impossible for the Dutch to control international trade. Among these were the British Navigation Acts, which banned foreign ships from transporting goods from other countries to England or to its colonies. In time, these policies did have the effect of diminishing the Dutch, and so by 1720, they no longer dominated international commerce.

But what had happened in the 17th century to the Dutch set the stage for a series of debates in the 18th century and even beyond. Was it mere coincidence that the richest country in Europe was also the most religiously tolerant? Or to put it in more general terms, was there a link between capitalism and tolerance? How should moralists evaluate the spread of consumption and the public's taste for new commodities? Was that something to be welcomed, or was it something to be feared?

And then there was the question of which policies worked better in enhancing national power, free trade or protectionism? Toleration, luxury, trade policy. It's to those debates that we'll turn next.

Lecture Five
Capitalism and Toleration—Voltaire

Scope:

Voltaire (1694–1778) was the central figure in the early European Enlightenment. By writing accessibly about matters of public interest for an audience that purchased his books in the commercial market, Voltaire helped carve out the modern role of the intellectual. In his *Letters on England* (1734), much of which concerned the evils of religious intolerance, Voltaire laid out the argument that commerce provides a means through which people of different ultimate orientations can cooperate. His portrait of the London Exchange entailed the defense of what was then a highly controversial institution, connected to what historians call "the financial revolution," which allowed Britain to become the leading world power.

Outline

I. There was a deep connection between capitalism and Enlightenment in two senses.
   A. New commercial means of communication and places of sociability made the Enlightenment possible, leading to the formation of public opinion.
   B. Thinking about the implications of the spread of commerce was a focus of concern for many of the thinkers of the Enlightenment.

II. Voltaire embodied and helped create the new social role of the intellectual, or to use the 18th-century French term, the *philosophe*.
   A. Until the 18th century, writers had depended primarily on patronage, the largesse of the rich and powerful, to provide them with a living.
   B. The rise of the market for print loosened authors' direct dependence on powerful patrons, even while it increased their dependence on the tastes of the reading public.

C. "Public opinion" was a product of new institutions through which a mass of citizens could become familiar with questions of government, including reading clubs, coffeehouses, and journals of opinion.

III. Voltaire's significance for our topic comes from his legitimization of self-interest and his popularization of the notion that the pursuit of wealth through market activity had important political benefits.
   A. Voltaire's *Letters on England* (1734; also known as *The Philosophical Letters*) was a work of social and political criticism that marked the beginning of the French Enlightenment as a public force.
   B. He was drawn to England by commercial, intellectual, and personal motives.
   C. What Voltaire most valued about contemporary European civilization was the growing liberty of the individual from coercion, through greater government toleration of intellectual differences and, above all, through the rule of law.
   D. He lays out the arguments about the links between individual self-interest and public welfare, the notion that economic self-interest was not just a source of suspicion, but that with proper channeling it would have positive effects.

IV. Voltaire's *Letters* tied the importance of trying to reduce religious ferocity to arguments in favor of the market.
   A. He argued that the pursuit of economic self-interest through the market might serve as an antidote to religious zealotry and religious intolerance.
   B. His literary portrait of the London Stock Exchange in his *Letters* helped popularize one of the most important and lasting arguments in favor of capitalism.
   C. It was Voltaire's claim that religious enthusiasm was a primary source of discord, which at best led to injustice, at worst to civil war.
   D. The quest for economic gain, he argued, made people more willing to tolerate those with different views of ultimate salvation.

V. The London Exchange was part of what historians now call "the financial revolution," a new form of financial capitalism closely linked to the rise of the modern state and international transoceanic commerce.

  A. The trading on the London Exchange was mainly in government securities: bonds and treasury bills.

  B. In the course of the 18th century, Britain replaced Holland as the great commercial and naval power of the era, and one reason for that was the founding of the Bank of England in 1694.

  C. Wars were often decided by whichever government was the first to run out of money. Until the founding of the Bank of England, the government borrowed money from private moneylenders at a fairly high rate of interest because the government wasn't considered a particularly good credit risk.

  D. With shares of these great merchant companies like the East India Company, shares of the Bank of England, and also bonds and treasury bills, the government could borrow money instead of depending on private moneylenders.

  E. The emergence of this stable, public market for state debt was in many ways the most politically significant economic innovation of the age. It allowed the British government to borrow funds at far lower interest rates, which meant that in case of war the British government could supply its troops and its navy for longer than its competitors could.

  F. The advantages to English power and English commerce brought by this financial revolution are now widely acknowledged by historians. But at the time, the public reacted to the new institutions of finance with suspicion and even hostility.

VI. The entire stock exchange scene was written so as to upset the reader's expectations by inverting the accustomed hierarchy of values.

  A. Voltaire's scene is meant to suggest that the pursuit of wealth through the market is actually more commendable than religious commitment.

B. The notion that capitalism allows for the bridging and diminution of cultural and religious differences would later be picked up by liberal supporters of capitalism (who saw it as promoting cosmopolitanism), as well as by critics who saw it as eroding religious and national commitments.

Suggested Reading:

Voltaire, *Letters on England*.

Williams, *Voltaire: Political Writings*.

Muller, *The Mind and the Market*, chap. 2.

Hirschman, *The Passions and the Interests*.

Questions to Consider:

1. How plausible is Voltaire's portrait of human relations on the London Exchange?
2. Do trade and commerce tend to lead to more peaceful relations between people of different faiths?

Lecture Five—Transcript
Capitalism and Toleration—Voltaire

We now arrive at the 18th century, the era of the Enlightenment. This lecture focuses on the most famous figure of the Enlightenment, at least in his day, namely Voltaire, who was born in 1694 and who died in 1778.

There is a deep connection between capitalism and the Enlightenment, or better, between capitalism and the Enlightenments, since there were actually major differences in emphasis of the Enlightenment from country to country. Also, there were large internal differences within each national Enlightenment, as we'll see in the next lecture when we look at the debate between Voltaire and Rousseau over luxury.

There was a deep connection between capitalism and Enlightenment in two senses. First of all, new commercial means of communication and new commercial places of sociability made the Enlightenment possible because the Enlightenment wasn't just a set of ideas or of debates. It was also a series of institutions by which public matters came to be publicly discussed and debated, leading to the formation of what came to be called "public opinion."

One could say that the very idea that government policy should be a matter of widespread discussion and debate was a key Enlightenment idea. Public opinion, as we'll see, was created largely through commercial means and in commercial spaces.

The second way in which there's a close connection between capitalism and the Enlightenment is that thinking about the implications of the spread of commerce was a focus of concern for many of the thinkers of the Enlightenment. Voltaire embodied, and really helped create, the new social role of what we would now call the intellectual, what the French in the 18th century came to call the *philosophe*, or the British, the man of letters—that is to say, a writer who tries to influence matters of public interest through his writing.

Up until then, writers who sought to influence public matters were either clerics who were supported by their orders or lay writers who were supported by patronage, that is to say, the support of some wealthy or powerful person as in the case of Hobbes. The rise of the intellectual was made possible by the rise of a growing market for print. It was only within the course of Voltaire's life, and in large part through his example, that the independent man of letters and the phenomenon of public opinion came to exist. So the rise of the intellectual and the growth of public opinion went hand in hand.

The rise of the intellectual meant a change in the way in which intellectual life was funded. In the past, the intellectual, the writer, had depended on a patron. Now he became dependent on the market. Until the 18th century, writers had depended primarily on the largesse of the rich and powerful to provide them with a living. Patronage was a highly personal relationship between the patron and the object of his or her largesse. As the 18th century progressed, it became possible for the first time to actually earn a living as a writer by selling one's books to readers, and that was because of the development of a capitalist market for books. Books increasingly made their way from the author to his readers through publishers and through booksellers who marketed the books. And so for the first time, it became possible to reach a mass of readers and to make a living, though usually a rather meager living, through the market for books.

The rise of this market for books loosened the author's direct dependence on powerful patrons. At the same time, it increased his dependence on the tastes of the reading public. If one wanted to make a living through selling one's books, then one had to write in a certain way. It depended not only on what one wrote, but how one wrote it. Here again, Voltaire is an exemplar. Both Voltaire's admirers and his critics agreed on the connection between his influence and the delight of his prose. Even Edmund Burke, who found Voltaire's influence maligned, conceded that, as he put it, "He has the merit of writing agreeably; and nobody has ever united blasphemy and obscenity so happily together."

Public opinion, then, was a product of new institutions through which a mass of citizens could become familiar with questions of government. Those new institutions included reading clubs, where men who couldn't afford to buy many books individually could gather together to read and discuss new works. Coffeehouses played a similar function. It's a place where one would come to drink coffee, to talk—and the coffeehouses were stocked with newspapers and journals that provided material to talk about, and they provided another setting where new ideas were disseminated.

Among the most important new forms of expression in the 18th century was the journal of opinion, which popularized ideas and reported on matters of public interest to a larger audience. The first such journal was *The Spectator*, which was founded in England in 1711, with the aim, as its editor put it, of bringing philosophy out of closets and libraries to dwell in clubs and assemblies.

Voltaire's great talent was as a popularizer of ideas that had first been developed by others, rather than as an original or systematic thinker. And Voltaire's significance for our topic comes from his popularization of two important themes: first of all, the legitimacy of material consumption and material improvement, a theme that we'll explore in the next lecture, and second, the notion that the pursuit of wealth through market activity had important political benefits. That theme he developed in his book of 1734, the *Letters on England*, a work of social and political criticism that marked the beginning of the French Enlightenment as a public force.

The book was loosely based on a trip that Voltaire actually took to England, where he spent two years, from 1726 to 1728. Voltaire was drawn to England by commercial motives, by intellectual motives, and by personal motives. Let's start with the commercial motive.

Voltaire had written an epic poem about Henry IV, the 16th-century French king who had granted toleration to the Protestants and had temporarily brought an end to religious war. And in this poem, Voltaire praised Henry for his toleration of religious differences. At the same time, he subjected the Catholic Church to a biting critique as a source of religious fanaticism. That criticism made the book subject to censorship in France, and the only way to publish it despite censorship was clandestinely, that is to say, without official permission. But that meant that the author would get almost none of the profits. Whatever profits there were would go almost entirely to the publisher, who assumed the risk of publishing this illegally. So one of Voltaire's motives for going to England was to arrange for the legal publication there of a deluxe edition of his poem, where the profits would go almost entirely to him.

He also had a personal reason for wanting to go to England, and that was to get out of prison. But the fact that Voltaire was in prison shows how little legal equality there was in France at the time. Here's what happened: Voltaire, already a well-known figure in Parisian circles, was at the Paris opera. There he was slighted by a leading nobleman, and Voltaire responded with a clever comment. The nobleman responded after the opera by having his servants beat Voltaire up. Voltaire then vowed to get his revenge. He started to take sword-fighting lessons. He bought pistols to prepare for a duel. Word got around that Voltaire was going to attack this leading French nobleman, and the government had Voltaire arrested and imprisoned in the Bastille. They finally agreed to release him with the promise that he'd get out of the country, that he'd leave for England. So that was a prompting motive as well.

Voltaire also had an intellectual motive. What Voltaire valued most about 18th-century European civilization was the growing liberty of the individual from coercion, through greater government toleration of intellectual differences, and above all, through the rule of law. By that standard, England was a model for the rest of Europe. Voltaire wanted to see it for himself, and he wanted to use England as a way of instructing the French about the benefits of greater liberty.

The problem of how people of differing faiths could live together without oppressing one another absorbed Voltaire when he arrived in England in 1726. And the product of his trip was a short book on England that would come to be known under its French title, the *Lettres Philosophiques*, *The Philosophical Letters*. It took the form of a book by a French traveler in England, a book intended for his countrymen back in France. And in the *Letters*, Voltaire lays out in the most straightforward terms the arguments about the links between individual self-interest and public welfare that had been suggested by Hobbes and by other 17th-century writers—the notion that economic self-interest was not just the source of suspicion, but that with proper channeling it would have positive effects.

Here's what Voltaire writes in the *Letters on England*:

> It is as impossible for a society to be formed and lasting without self-interest as it would be to produce children without carnal desire or to think of eating without appetite, etc. It is love of self that encourages love of others, it is through our mutual needs that we become useful to the human race. That is the foundation of all commerce, the eternal link between men. ... It is quite true that God might have created beings solely concerned with the good of others. In that case merchants would have gone out to the Indies out of charity and the mason would have cut stone to

give pleasure to his neighbor. But God has ordained things differently. Let us not condemn the instinct He has given us, and let us put it to the use He commands.

Here we see a wonderful example of Voltaire's popularization of that theme of the possible social benefits of self-love and self-interest, which we saw in one way in Hobbes in the 17th century and another in Pierre Nicole.

Another theme that Voltaire took from Hobbes was the importance of trying to reduce religious ferocity. But now Voltaire tied that theme to arguments in favor of the market. Voltaire argued that the pursuit of economic self-interest through the market might serve as an antidote to religious zealotry and religious intolerance. We see that most clearly in Voltaire's literary portrait of the London Exchange in these *Letters on England*. There, he helped popularize one of the most important and lasting arguments in favor of capitalism, and that was Voltaire's defense of the market as conducive to toleration, an argument that was as much political as economic.

It was Voltaire's claim that religious enthusiasm was the primary source of social discord, which at best led to injustice and at worst led to civil war. In the English *Letters*, he loses no opportunity to hammer home his contention that religious wars are senseless since they're rooted in theological questions to which no definitive or even plausible answers can be given. That's also a popularization of ideas that are already in Hobbes.

Voltaire's portrait of England in his *Letters on England* record and applaud the passing of religious fanaticism and its replacement by an atmosphere of religious toleration. One reason for that, Voltaire thought, was the displacement of religious concerns by the pursuit of wealth and the pursuit of happiness. The quest for economic gain, he shows in his description of the London Exchange, made men more willing to tolerate one another, made men more willing to tolerate people with different views of ultimate salvation. Here is Voltaire's description:

> Come into the London Exchange, a place more respectable than many a court. You will see assembled representatives of every nation for the benefit of mankind. Here the Jew, the Mohametan and the Christian deal with one another as if

they were of the same religion, and reserve the name "infidel" for those who go bankrupt. Here the Presbyterian puts his trust in the Anabaptist, and the Anglican accepts the Quaker's promissory note. Upon leaving these peaceful and free assemblies, one goes to the synagogue, the other for a drink; yet another goes to have himself baptized in a large tub in the name of the Father through the Son to the Holy Ghost; another has his son's foreskin cut off, and over the infant he has muttered some Hebrew words that he doesn't understand at all: Some others go to their church to await divine inspiration with their hat on their heads. And all are content.

Notice what Voltaire is trying to suggest here: that while religious enthusiasm would lead these people to damn one another as infidels, to be at one another's throat, the quest for wealth creates a new consensus, creates a new basis for cooperation across religious lines. They all agree that in the setting of the London Exchange it's the bankrupt, and he alone, who is unfaithful, who is an infidel. So Voltaire is trying to suggest to us that compared to the competitive quest for salvation that often leads to strife and antagonism, the quest for wealth is more likely to make men peaceful and, he even claims, content.

What was the London Exchange? What were these merchants buying and selling? Voltaire's setting of this scene in favor of toleration on the London Exchange takes on even greater power when we put it in its historical context, because the London Exchange was the embodiment, at the time, of a new form of financial capitalism. It was one embodiment of a set of institutions that historians now call "the financial revolution," and that they recognized as one of the prerequisites for British economic and political success in the 18th century and thereafter. But in their day, these new institutions were very controversial. They were decried by moralists, and we'll see why.

Let's take a closer look at the forms of commerce that Voltaire was defending, at the forms of commerce that were going on on the London Exchange. What was it that was being exchanged? Well, there was trading in shares of the great charter companies, shares in the Bank of England, shares in new forms of government securities: bonds and treasury bills.

Let's start with the chartered companies. These were companies like the East India Company or the South Sea Company. This sort of company, you will recall, had been pioneered by the Dutch—remember the Dutch East India Company. They were chartered by the government, and they were given a monopoly, that is to say, an exclusive right to import goods from one or another designated region of the world—India, the South Seas, parts of the New World, and so on. These companies were owned in part by royal investors and in part by private shareholders, who shared the risks by investing their capital and who hoped, of course, to share in the profits.

In the course of the 18th century, Britain had replaced Holland as the great commercial and the great naval power of the era. One reason for that was the founding of the Bank of England, shares of which were also being traded on the London Exchange. Indeed, the founding of the Bank of England in 1694 was another key element of this financial revolution. Now you'll ask, what could banking and military power have to do with one another? The answer is, a great deal. Up till then, wars were often decided by whichever government was the first to run out of money with which to pay its troops. Like most of European governments of the day, the British government's expenditures usually exceeded its revenues, and until the late 17th century and the founding of the Bank of England, the government of England usually raised its revenues in a way that was typical of the time—the way it was typical in France and other continental countries—and that is, first of all, that when its revenues were smaller than its expenditures, the government simply borrowed money from private moneylenders to cover the government's expenses, to cover the government deficit.

This system was really quite expensive. The government had to pay a lot in order to borrow the money because the government borrowed money at the same rate of interest as did private individuals. And the government had to pay a fairly high rate of interest because the government wasn't considered a particularly good credit risk, and that was because not only were its revenues often less than its expenditures, but the government had a very inefficient and rather unreliable way of raising tax revenues, and that was through essentially private tax collectors.

Here is how it worked: The government sold the right to collect one or another form of taxes to a person called a "tax farmer." The tax farmer would bid on the right to collect taxes, say, on sweet wine. These were excise taxes. The tax farmer had to promise to pay a stipulated amount to the government, and whatever the tax farmer could take in in revenue that was greater than the amount that he had to pay the government belonged to him. In other words, he had an incentive to extract as much as he could from the population.

This was an inefficient and a rather expensive way of paying for government expenses, and in the late 17th century, the British government replaced this system of borrowing from moneylenders and of collecting revenue through tax farmers. It did so by imitating a method of government funding, of funding government debt, that had been pioneered by the Dutch, and that was the establishment of a national bank, in this case, the Bank of England. The Bank of England—and its name might seem a bit deceptive in this regard—the Bank of England was a private, chartered company, and it began its existence, and indeed, it was given its charter, in order to provide the government with money—a lot of money, £1.2 million, which in those days was a lot of money—in return for which the government promised to pay the Bank of England an annual sum of £100,000 in perpetuity, forever. And it also permitted the Bank of England to receive deposits, to make loans, and to issue bank notes.

The stockholders of the Bank of England included the king—and remember, in terms of his religious affiliation, the king was the head of the Church of England. It included merchants and bankers from London, some of whom were from the dissenting sects who were outside of the Church of England. The investors included French Calvinists refugees, the Huguenots, and the investors included some Jews who had recently been allowed back into England after having been expelled from there in the late Middle Ages. And the investors included Dutch investors as well. So you'll notice the varied religious and national backgrounds of these investors active on the London Exchange, in this case, through investing in the Bank of England.

What was being traded on the London Exchange? Were shares of these great merchant companies like the East India Company, shares of the Bank of England, and also new financial instruments through which the government could borrow from the private money market? Those financial instruments were bonds and treasury bills through which the government could now borrow money instead of depending on private moneylenders.

In the case of these bonds and treasury bills, the government promised to pay some face amount at a future date, and it promised to pay a fixed annual interest until the bill became due. So the government's ability to sell these bonds and treasury bills—that is to say, the government's ability to borrow from the private market—depended on the belief of investors that the government had the capacity to meet these payments, that it could meet the annual interest payments, and that it would eventually be in a position to pay back the face value of the bonds and bills when they came due.

Increasingly, investors had that confidence, and that was because the British government had developed a new and much more effective system of collecting taxes. Instead of relying on these private tax farmers, the government developed its own bureaucracy to collect taxes. The main way that it had available to it to collect taxes was to collect taxes on imports. That was the easiest thing for the government to tax. The development of this governmental bureaucracy to collect taxes regularly provided the government with a substantial and regular flow of funds into government coffers.

That increased the confidence of investors in the government. It meant that lending money to the government was one of the least risky sorts of investments that one could make, and therefore investors required a low rate of interest from the government since the risk was seen as quite minimal. And that tremendously increased the spending capacity of the British government. So the emergence of this stable, public market for state debt was in many ways the most politically significant economic innovation of the age. It allowed the British government, then, to borrow funds at a far lower rate than had been the case in the past, and that meant that in case of war the British government could supply its troops and its navy for longer than its competitors could. So there was a strong connection between Britain's new financial institutions and its growing military power.

The development of these new means of finance had important economic consequences, too. As more investment capital flowed into London from elsewhere in Britain and from other countries, as more capital was available, interest rates fell. That made it easier for businesses to borrow more money at lower interest rates in order to start new business ventures or to expand them.

In historical retrospect, the advantages to English power and to English commerce brought about by this financial revolution, they're now widely acknowledged by historians. But at the time, the public reacted to these new institutions of finance with suspicion and even with hostility. It was said that these investors on the floor of the London Exchange were mere moneygrubbers, that they were speculators, that they were gamblers, that they were half insane, that they were taking their money out of secure investments like land, which was considered the most stable and secure investment one could have, and putting it into dubious investments that depended on people's imagination, people's fantasy, or so it was said, because it depended on people's estimate of things like how well the East India Company was doing, what rumors were there about how its ships were doing at sea. It depended on people's estimates of the creditworthiness of the government. All of this was seen as a product of, or influenced by, the imagination as lacking the solidity of traditional investments in the land.

So as you can see, Voltaire's entire London Exchange scene was written to upset the reader's expectations, to turn those expectations on its head. In public discussions, this buying and selling of stock on the London Exchange was often depicted as the depths of self-seeking. But Voltaire describes those engaged in trading as pursuing the benefit of mankind.

The key inversion of the accepted hierarchy of values, of course, concerns business and religion, or the pursuit of wealth compared to the quest for salvation. The traditional assumption would have been that the quest for salvation is high and commendable; the quest for wealth is low and ignoble. Voltaire turns that evaluation on its head. Voltaire's scene is meant to suggest that the pursuit of wealth through the market is actually more commendable than religious commitment.

The notion that capitalism allows for the bridging and diminution of cultural and religious differences would later be picked up by many liberal supporters of capitalism. They saw the diminution of religious differences as promoting toleration. They saw the bridging of national differences as promoting cosmopolitanism, greater humanitarianism—larger than one's own nation. This idea that market relations are conducive to diminishing religious commitments and national commitments would prove to be a two-edged sword because these arguments were also picked up by critics of capitalism. They were picked up by religious critics who saw capitalism as eroding religious commitments. Well, Voltaire saw that too. But of course, for those who were religiously committed, the fact that market relations might diminish religious commitment was a very negative thing, a very worrisome phenomenon.

Similarly, nationalist critics took up this notion that capitalist relations erode a commitment to one's particular nation, and they saw that as a very negative and worrisome phenomenon as well. Even within the Enlightenment itself, there was dissent from the view that the spread of commerce and finance and the new goods that they were making available was something necessarily to be welcomed.

In the next lecture, we'll turn to the debate between Voltaire and his foremost critic within the Enlightenment, Jean-Jacques Rousseau.

Lecture Six
Abundance or Equality—Voltaire vs. Rousseau

Scope:

A major debate during the Enlightenment concerned the moral status of material well-being. Moralists in the civic and Christian traditions stigmatized material comfort as "luxury." Voltaire laid out a number of arguments in defense of luxury: that the very notion of what constituted "luxury" was historically relative, and that luxury was the basis of civilization. His arguments were countered by Jean-Jacques Rousseau, who argued that material progress had increased inequality, undermined virtue, and actually made people less happy.

Outline

I. In two works published shortly after his *Letters on England*, Voltaire set forth another defense of commerce: that it promoted material wealth and comfort.
   A. In the 18th century, material prosperity was frequently condemned as "luxury" by religious and civic moralists.
   B. Moralists in the civic tradition saw luxury as leading to the decline of nations.
   C. Christian moralists portrayed luxury as distracting men and women from the pursuit of salvation.

II. Voltaire and other leading thinkers of the Enlightenment reacted against a political culture based on the aristocratic values of manliness and warfare, and against a religious culture oriented to piety.
   A. In its place, they endorsed an emerging secular culture that valued gentler relations of sociability.
   B. They worked to bring about a culture in which people's imaginations were filled not by stories of religious miracles or experiences of ascetic piety or the contemplation of the mysteries of faith. Instead they sought to fill the imagination through secular art, literature, histories, and the wonders of natural science.

- C. That was what Voltaire and Hume meant by "civilization": a world of arts and sciences, of technological improvement and greater well-being.
- D. The material basis of that world, they argued, came from the economic growth brought about by commerce. Luxury to them meant the increased possibilities for consumption and leisure brought about by economic growth.

III. Voltaire entered the debate over luxury in 1736, with the distribution of his poem "The Worldling."
- A. It combined its praise of contemporary worldly joys with ridicule of the Christian and civic myths of past golden ages.
- B. He argued that material prosperity is the prerequisite for the development of higher civilization.
- C. Voltaire defended luxury against its moralist detractors by trying to show that the notion was historically relative: that much of what his contemporaries considered to be basic necessities had once been regarded as luxuries.
- D. He later developed this point in his *Philosophical Dictionary*, with his example that when scissors were first invented they were called a luxury for "dandies and squanderers" who used them to "mar the work of the Creator."
- E. Voltaire's defense of consumption was echoed by other great figures of the Enlightenment, including Scottish philosopher David Hume, but it came under attack by another figure of the Enlightenment, Jean-Jacques Rousseau.

IV. Rousseau became the most important internal critic of the Enlightenment, critical of key trends in Enlightenment thought.
- A. His breakthrough to fame came in 1750, in his "Discourse on the Arts and Sciences," followed by his "Discourse on Inequality" in 1755.
- B. Rousseau not only denied that progress in the arts and sciences improves morality, he asserted, on the contrary, that such progress leads to moral corruption.
- C. The arts (by which he also meant the fine arts and the mechanical arts) and sciences, Rousseau argued, bring with them the desire for unnecessary wants and comforts that distract people from their moral purposes.

- D. Indeed, people will sacrifice political freedom and self-rule in order to pursue the comforts and stimuli offered by the arts and by luxury. They become "happy slaves," so besotted by culture and luxury that they don't recognize their servile state.
- V. The development of the arts and sciences also leads to inequality, with negative moral consequences.
  - A. The talents needed to pursue the arts and sciences are unequally distributed among people, and in a civilized society this becomes the basis of greater distinction among people.
  - B. In addition, a civilized society demands great expenditure to support those who distinguish themselves in the arts and sciences, and this can only come about when some work for others, leading to greater inequality.
  - C. Thus in modern commercial nations there is a gap between the rich and the poor, and that comes at the expense of the self-esteem of the poor.
  - D. Calculation of self-interest becomes the basis of human relations, and this destroys the foundations of trust and leads to poor citizenship.
- VI. The great corruption of human sentiments comes with the creation of private property.
  - A. With the notion of private property comes the fact that some people have more private property and some people have less.
  - B. It leads to inequality: Because people have different talents, some of them increase their possessions, and soon some have more than they need and others less.
  - C. A state of war ensues between the haves and the have-nots.
  - D. It also leads to alienation, as people come to live for others, as they learn to compare themselves with them.
  - E. As people move into civilization and as civilization develops, people's desires grow—especially the desire for the recognition of other people—and so man becomes driven by his vanity, his *amour-propre*.

- **F.** Because there is scarcity and the needs and desires of all people in society cannot be satisfied, the rich need protection and the poor are oppressed.
- **G.** As an antidote to the corruptions of modern society, Rousseau sought a reinvigorated civic republicanism.

VII. Who was right, Voltaire or Rousseau?
- **A.** Do our increasing comforts, made possible by economic growth, make us happier, as Voltaire suggests?
- **B.** Or is Rousseau right? Isn't all this a distraction from some higher purpose?
- **C.** If, as Rousseau believes, what we long for is the recognition of others, and if recognition is a zero-sum game, then isn't inequality too high a price to pay for material improvement?
- **D.** This line of thought is continued in the 20th-century conception of poverty as "relative deprivation."

Suggested Reading:

Clark, *Commerce, Culture and Liberty* (Voltaire, "The Worldling," "The Man of the World," "Of Commerce and Luxury"; Rousseau, "Luxury, Commerce and the Arts").

Rousseau, *The Discourses and Other Early Political Writings*.

Questions to Consider:

1. Who do you think is more correct about the moral effects of economic growth, Voltaire or Rousseau?
2. Are contemporary citizens motivated more by concern with the economic well-being of the nation or their own, narrower economic well-being? Should the government try to cultivate civic-mindedness in its citizens?

Lecture Six—Transcript
Abundance or Equality—Voltaire vs. Rousseau

In his *Letters on England*, those philosophical letters, Voltaire had defended the market as an antidote to religious fanaticism through its promotion of peaceful, self-interested cooperation. In two poems published shortly thereafter called "The Worldling" and the "Defence of the Worldling," he set forth a second defense of commerce, that it promoted material wealth and comfort.

Well, you might ask, what was controversial about that? What was there to argue about? To us, the argument in favor of material well-being probably seems uncontroversial, but in the 18th century it wasn't. Material prosperity was frequently condemned as luxury by religious and civic moralists. Luxury wasn't a morally neutral word. It was a pejorative, connoting not comfort, but excess, the possession of nonnecessities.

Moralists in the civic tradition saw luxury as leading to the decline of nations. The richer the commonwealth became, it was said, the greater would be the pursuit of individual material satisfactions at the expense of the common good. They alleged that material comfort made men soft and effeminate. They said that nations that pursued luxury would be defeated by the armies of more austere, virtuous, manly, and warlike nations.

Christian moralists had a different critique of luxury. They portrayed luxury as distracting men and women from the pursuit of salvation. There was a long Christian tradition of interpreting virtue in ascetic terms, in terms of abstinence, privation, and humility. These were the qualities of character that it was thought desirable to cultivate. These kinds of character traits were what the Scottish philosopher David Hume dismissed as "the monkish virtues," which he, like many Enlightenment figures, thought were not properly virtues at all because they weren't oriented to this-worldly activity; they were oriented toward otherworldly contemplation.

Though Hume was very much of a non-Christian, he was right that abstinence, privation (also known as poverty), and humility were, indeed, Christian virtues, and that these virtues were very much at odds with the promotion of worldly comfort. In *The City of God*, Augustine had warned that prosperity begets luxury and then avarice.

And later Christian thinkers warned time and again that luxury bound the flesh to the world and to the devil.

So both the civic and the Christian traditions condemned the pursuit of material wealth, though for different reasons. The civic tradition saw it as corrupting the virtuous citizen, who ought to be prepared to sacrifice his private concerns for those of the state, thus defending the commonwealth in war and bringing him glory. The Christian tradition saw material comfort as a temptation to sin, leading away from godliness and the virtues of abstinence, humility, and love.

Voltaire and other leading thinkers of the Enlightenment reacted against a political culture that was based, on the one hand, on these aristocratic virtues of manliness, warfare, and fighting. And they were also revolting against a religious culture that was oriented toward piety. In place of those, they endorsed an emerging secular culture, and one that valued gentler relations of sociability, the sort that one would find at the salon, or the coffeehouse, or in the theater, or in the library, and they looked for guidance, not to religion, but to philosophy and to science.

The main thinkers of the Enlightenment worked to bring about a culture in which people's imaginations were filled not by stories of religious miracles or experiences of ascetic piety or the contemplation of the mysteries of faith. Instead, they sought to fill the imagination with secular art, secular literature—that's one reason that they wrote novels—secular histories, and the wonders of natural science. That was what Voltaire and David Hume meant by "civilization": a world of arts and sciences, of technological improvement and greater well-being. And the material basis for that world, they argued, came from the economic growth brought about by commerce. Luxury, to them, meant the increased possibilities for consumption and leisure brought about by economic growth, and they welcomed it with open arms.

Voltaire entered this debate in 1736, with the distribution of a poem called "The Worldling," or "the man of the world." The poem began: "I thank wise nature that led me to be born in this age, so decried by our poor Doctors," by which he meant the doctors of the church. This poem was a hymn in praise of contemporary urban luxury, and it was an attack on the Christian virtue of self-denial and on the civic republican virtue of frugality. In it, Voltaire combined his praise of contemporary worldly joys with the ridicule of the Christian and civic myths of past golden ages. He satirized the Christian conception that there was a primeval paradise before civilization. The state of nature, he wrote, was very far from being Edenic, and in a very humorous passage, he pictures Adam and Eve in their primeval garden, their faces without protection and burned by the sun, their hands scaly, their uncut nails long, cracked, black, and hooked, their couplings almost animal-like. What was so ideal, he asked, about a situation without the comforts of 18th-century Paris?

And then he took aim at the civic republican myth of ancient Roman virtue. He insisted that the life of the ancient Romans was characterized not by the vaunted virtue of frugality. That was a nice way of putting it, but in fact, he said, they were poor, uncomfortable, and ignorant, which had nothing admirable about it. And so Voltaire ridiculed the civic and the Christian versions of the good old days, unspoiled by decadent luxury. "Abundance is the mother of the arts," wrote Voltaire in his poem, and he argued that material prosperity is the prerequisite for the development of higher civilization.

Another way in which Voltaire defended luxury against its moralistic detractors was by trying to relativize the notion by trying to show that the notion was historically relative, to show that much of what his contemporaries considered to be basic necessities had once been regarded as extraordinary, as luxuries. He develops this point again with typical wit in his *Philosophical Dictionary*, written some years later. Here's what he says:

> When scissors, which surely do not date from remote antiquity, were invented, what wasn't said against the first people who used them to clip their nails, and who cut some of the hair that fell down over their noses? They were doubtless called dandies and squanderers, who bought an expensive instrument of vanity to mar the work of the Creator.

Voltaire's defense of consumption was echoed by some of the other great figures of the Enlightenment, for example, the Scottish philosopher David Hume. But it came under attack by another figure of the Enlightenment, Jean-Jacques Rousseau. Let's turn, then, to Rousseau.

What a character. Rousseau was born in 1712, the son of an itinerant watchmaker from Geneva. He worked in a variety of occupations, first for a while as an engraver, as a music copyist. In 1742, so when he was about 30, he moved to Paris, and there he began a career as a writer. One of those people who he befriended was Denis Diderot, who would become the editor of the *Encyclopédie* (the *Encyclopedia*), the great compendium of French Enlightenment thought, a compendium that was intended to combine useful knowledge about everything from agriculture to manufacturing, and to combine them with enlightened reflections on social and political issues.

While walking to Vincennes on the outskirts of Paris to meet Diderot, Rousseau had a moment of insight, which he later described in these words. His insight was "that man is naturally good, and that it is by his institutions alone that men become evil."

Rousseau's life was full of paradox. He was an advocate of family intimacy, who early in his life, from the years when he was 15 until he was about 25, had had a decade-long affair with a married woman he called "Mama." Thereafter, he lived with another woman with whom he had a number of children who they handed over to an orphanage.

An advocate of friendship, he quarreled with many of his fellow *philosophes*. Indeed, he became the most important internal critic of the Enlightenment—part of the Enlightenment, but critical of key trends in Enlightenment thought.

Rousseau's breakthrough to fame came in 1750. That year the Academy of Dijon sponsored a contest for the best essay to answer the question "Has the reestablishment of the arts and sciences contributed to the purification or the corruption of morals?" That was the question. Of course, the standard enlightened answer would be that it had, indeed, contributed to the purification of morals and to human moral improvement. Rousseau's answer, in this famous "Discourse on the Arts and Sciences," was that the progress of the arts and sciences had led to the corruption of morals.

Rousseau won the contest, not least for his boldness in answering the question negatively in such a counterintuitive way given the atmosphere of the Enlightenment. Rousseau went on in his subsequent works to argue that modern society was based upon a way of life precisely contrary to what would make people happy.

In 1755, he wrote a second famous essay, the "Discourse on Inequality." That one didn't win the contest, but it was probably even more important in terms of intellectual history. There, he argued that society as it was now constituted had no claim on the moral adhesion of its subjects—indeed, that contemporary commercial society was fundamentally immoral.

When we compare Rousseau to Voltaire, or to Hume, we see that Rousseau is divided from these other members of the Enlightenment by a gap. Voltaire, Hume, most other figures in the Enlightenment had seen the spread of commerce as an essentially positive and benevolent force, not least because it created the preconditions for greater material comfort, and for the development of the arts and sciences, and for relations between people that were more peaceful and that were an antidote to religious conflict.

With Rousseau we see many of these valuations reversed. Rousseau shared the Enlightenment's bottom line, its lowest common conceptual denominator, so to speak—that is, the commitment to increasing worldly happiness. That he shared with his fellow members of the Enlightenment. But he thought that many of the methods and institutions advocated by Voltaire and other enlightened intellectuals actually made people less happy.

Rousseau's guiding terms were equality, moral virtue, and he saw both of those as having been corrupted by the modern world. Let's look at Rousseau's arguments in these two essays on how the progress of civilization has actually made people less happy. Rousseau not only denies that progress in the arts and sciences improves morality, he asserts, on the contrary, that such progress actually leads to moral corruption. Here's a taste of his argument, and I quote here:

> Princes always view with pleasure the spread, among their subjects, of the taste for pleasant arts and luxuries. ... For, in addition to nurturing in them that pettiness of soul so appropriate to servitude, princes know very well that all the needs the populace imposes on itself are so many chains which burden it.
>
> [The] letters, and arts [he writes] spread garlands of flowers over the iron chains with which men are burdened, stifle in them the sense of that original liberty for which they seemed

to have been born, make them love their slavery, and turn them into what is called civilized peoples.

And he means this term "civilized" ironically. Rousseau is claiming here that the arts, by which he means not only the fine arts—not only literature, painting, music, and so on—but also the mechanical arts and the sciences, that these arts and sciences bring with them the desire for new wants, new comforts, and that this desire for new wants and new comforts actually distracts people from moral purposes and from their desire for political participation.

If virtue is understood politically as participation in the search for the common good, in the willingness to put common interests above individual interests, in the willingness to sacrifice oneself for the sake of the polity, in the need for the citizen to participate in his own governance rather than being ruled over by the prince, then the development of the arts and sciences tends to make us less virtuous, more concerned with our own comforts.

Indeed, Rousseau claims, men sacrifice their political freedom and that inward desire for self-rule in order to pursue the comforts and stimuli that are offered by luxury and offered by the arts. That's the sense in which, as Rousseau puts it, they come to love their slavery; that is, they don't notice their lack of political freedom, their lack of self-determination, because they're so caught up with the pursuit and enjoyment of material comforts. Or because cultural and intellectual matters so fascinate them that they stop thinking about issues of politics. They stop thinking about themselves as self-determining citizens. In short, they are what Rousseau calls "happy slaves," so besotted by culture and luxury that they don't recognize their own servile state.

The development of the arts and sciences has another negative consequence as well, according to Rousseau, and that is that it leads to greater inequality, and that's because, Rousseau says, the talents needed to pursue the various arts and sciences are unequally distributed among men. Some do better than others, and in a civilized society, this becomes the basis of greater distinction among people, the fact that some have excelled in the arts and letters and sciences, and some have done less well.

In addition, he says, a civilized society with all those academies, all those universities, all those theaters, all those music halls, all those libraries, all those places in which the arts and sciences are pursued, a civilized society demands great expenditure to support those who distinguish themselves in the arts and sciences. And this can only come about, Rousseau says, when some people do the work so that others can engage in these kinds of higher processes, and that leads to another sort of inequality. And so, he says, in modern nations characterized by commerce and by the arts and sciences, there's a gap between the rich and the poor, and that gap comes at the expense of the self-esteem of the poor.

Money, he says, has become the standard of human worth, and virtue is forgotten. Calculations of self-interest have become the basis of human relationships, and this destroys, he says, the foundations of trust and leads to poor citizenship. As he famously put it, "What will become of virtue when one must become wealthy at any cost? Ancient politicians spoke incessantly about mores and virtue; ours speak only of commerce and money." The challenge, then, as Rousseau conceives of it, is for intellectuals and rulers to lead people back to virtue.

What Rousseau regards as the great corruption of human sentiments, his secular equivalent of a fall of man, comes with the creation of private property, which he said came about as men moved from primitive nomadism, where they didn't have property, to settled agriculture. The man who brought the greatest evils to mankind, Rousseau says, was the one who first said, "This land belongs to me," because with the cultivation of the land comes the notion of private property, and with it comes the fact that some people have more private property and some people have less. So with it comes inequality, again because people have different talents, and that leads some of them to increase their possessions so that soon enough they have more than they need, and there are others whose talents don't allow them to acquire possessions. Perhaps they don't have the talents, and so they have less than they need. In Rousseau's accounting, that leads to a situation in which a state of war ensues between the haves and the have-nots, and that is the basis of the contract that leads to the creation of government, a contract that really protects the rich from the poor.

This gap between the rich and the poor—that is to say, the gap created by inequality—for Rousseau is one source of man's misery. The other source is that man in a civilized society comes increasingly to live for others. In that sense, this is a theory of alienation. He comes to live for others in the sense, first of all, that as he moves into society, he's now physically dependent upon other people. Secondly, and more importantly, he comes to live for others in the sense that he learns to compare himself with other people, and he constantly does so and is dissatisfied when he has less than they do.

As people move into civilization and as civilization develops, according to Rousseau, people's desires grow, especially the desire for the recognition of other people. And so man becomes driven by what Rousseau calls his vanity, his *amour-propre*. His needs, which in primitive society were very limited, now become open-ended, unlimited. He's possessed by infinite yearnings for possessions that he doesn't really need. And here's the really dissatisfying part, the part that really makes him unhappy: He can never get enough of what he most craves, and that is the recognition of others.

Because there is scarcity and the needs and desires of all men in society can't be satisfied, the rich need protection and the poor are oppressed. Hobbes, Rousseau thought, was right in saying that men found civil society because of the hostility engendered by their infinite desires, but he says those desires are not part of man's innate nature. They are a product of man's social state, of the development of private property, of the development of commerce, of the development of the arts and sciences. So what for Hobbes seemed like the solution, to Rousseau is really the problem.

As an antidote to the corruptions of modern society, Rousseau looked back to ancient models, ancient Greece, ancient Rome, and especially to the favorite model in the civic republican tradition, to ancient Sparta. That is to say, he wanted to reinvigorate, re-create the civic republican tradition. He wanted a circumstance in which part of that civic activity was for people to play a role again in governing themselves collectively so that the people who made the rules and the people who obeyed the rules were one in the same. In that sense, he is a theorist of modern democracy.

Education, he said, shouldn't be the kind of education that the Enlightenment typically promoted. It shouldn't be an education in the arts, shouldn't be an education in the sciences, shouldn't be an education in philosophy. It should be primarily a moral education. That's a theme that he explored in his great book on education, the *Émile*.

The primary consideration of a government, Rousseau said, should be the virtue of its citizens, not their material comfort, not the progress of the arts and sciences. It should be the virtue of the citizens, where virtue is defined as concern for the common good, their willingness to put common interests above individual interests, their willingness to sacrifice themselves, if necessary, for the sake of the polity. These are some of the ideas that Rousseau articulated in his later work of 1762, *The Social Contract*.

Those ideas he thought could only be realized in a relatively small polity, and in a polity with private property but with a considerable degree of equality. So for Rousseau, that's the preferred state, a small group of self-governing people with a substantial degree of equality. That's the solution.

Who is right, Voltaire or Rousseau? Do our increasing comforts, made possible by economic growth, make us happier as Voltaire suggests? Should we be grateful to be born in modern times? Should we be grateful to be born in the 20th century and not at some time in the past where society was poor, medicine was less developed, and most of the cultural possibilities that we take for granted—from recorded music to recorded lectures—where those cultural possibilities didn't exist? Isn't economic growth the basis of scientific development, of medical improvements that have made our lives longer and less pain-ridden? That's Voltaire's argument.

Or, is Rousseau right? Isn't all of this science, isn't all of this literature, isn't all of this entertainment, isn't all of this material comfort, isn't all of this a distraction from some higher purpose? Is Rousseau right that the development of commercial society leads our appetites to grow faster than the means to fulfill them, so that we're constantly wanting more and we're never really satisfied?

If competition leads to inequality of attainment, which Rousseau says is inevitable because, after all, people aren't equal in their talents, then does inequality of attainment itself doom most of us to unhappiness? If what we long for is the recognition of others as the smartest, richest, most beautiful, most successful, and if recognition is a zero-sum game—that is to say, if it's a situation where if I get more recognition, you get less—then isn't inequality too high a price to pay for these material improvements, for living in a commercial society?

This debate over inequality continues on into the 20th century. One of Rousseau's key ideas has been reformulated in the 20th century with the conception of poverty as "relative deprivation." There the notion is it's not how much people have absolutely that matters, it's the fact that some people have more than others that's bothersome because those who have less feel relatively deprived compared to those who have more.

Or, as Voltaire and Hume responded to Rousseau, isn't Rousseau's obsession with equality a recipe for collective poverty? How can we promote achievement if we decry the situation when the outcomes of achievement are unequal?

At the conclusion of his discourse on inequality, Rousseau claimed that in commercial society the privileged few gorged themselves with superfluous things while the starving multitude lacked the bare necessities of life.

In Scotland, a young moral philosopher wrote a review of Rousseau's work, which he thought was rhetorically brilliant but wrongheaded. That moral philosopher was Adam Smith. First he wrote a book showing how what Rousseau had called vanity, *amour-propre*, the desire for recognition from others, was actually the basis of the development of conscience and of moral self-judgment. And then, Smith set about writing a book on political economy, a book that remains perhaps the single greatest book on capitalism.

We'll turn to him and to his book, *An Inquiry into the Nature and Causes of the Wealth of Nations*, in our next lecture.

Lecture Seven
Seeing the Invisible Hand—Adam Smith

Scope:

Adam Smith (1723–1790) began his career as a Professor of Moral Philosophy, and he took his moral concerns into his study of what he called "commercial society" and the new science of political economy. The goal of the market economy, as Smith conceived of it, was to make possible an ongoing rise in the standard of living of the vast majority of the population. In *The Wealth of Nations* (1776), he laid out a model that explained how a competitive market channeled self-interest in socially beneficial directions. It did so by increasing productivity and making commodities available at cheaper prices, affordable by ever-broader portions of the population. This is the famous "invisible hand"—a metaphor for institutional arrangements that channel self-interest toward socially desirable outcomes.

Outline

I. In this lecture, we'll look briefly at who Adam Smith was and at some of the key historical experiences that formed the backdrop of his writings on the market, especially the process that historians call the "consumer revolution" of 18th-century Britain.

    A. Smith's *Inquiry into the Nature and Causes of the Wealth of Nations* emerged out of his reflections upon the real successes of the consumer revolution.

    B. Smith was a Professor of Philosophy. He was born in Scotland in 1723, studied in Glasgow and Oxford, and was appointed to a Professorship of Philosophy at the University of Edinburgh.

    C. His first book, *The Theory of Moral Sentiments* (1759), sets out a social scientific explanation of how people become moral beings.

    D. Though Smith would later write a great deal about the role of self-interest in human affairs, he regarded the attempt to explain all of human action on the basis of self-interest or self-love as patently absurd.

II. One of the most important developments in 18th-century European life was the increasing role of commerce, and nowhere was this commercialization more evident than in the case of Smith's own Scotland.

   A. Across Europe, philosophers and "men of letters" in the 18th century were turning their attention to the spread of commerce and reflecting on its moral and political implications.

   B. Once Smith finished *The Theory of Moral Sentiments*, he too turned his attention to reflecting upon the implications of the growth of commerce.

   C. *The Wealth of Nations* was written against the background of what historians now call the "consumer revolution."

   D. Economic conditions in Britain were improving, slowly but demonstrably, and this provided the historical backdrop of the book.

III. In Smith's day, many policymakers viewed trade with other European powers as a form of undeclared warfare, with the object of maximizing benefits to England while minimizing those to rival nations.

   A. The prime weapons in this war were prohibitions on the import of goods, or heavy government duties on imported goods, which made them less profitable to bring into the country.

   B. The goal of Smith's analysis was to bring about "universal opulence," or a respectable standard of living for as many people as possible.

   C. Economic growth was hampered, in Smith's eyes, by existing protectionist restrictions, so much of *The Wealth of Nations* was an argument for expanding the freedom to trade.

   D. *The Wealth of Nations* was a work of political economy with two objectives: to provide plentiful subsistence to the people and to provide the state with sufficient revenue to cover the cost of public services.

   E. Smith lays out a couple of key models of the capitalist economy based on observation and on generalization from those observations.

IV. Smith sets out the first element of his model, which is self-interest as a motivating force in market activity.
  A. Smith does not claim that all of human relations is based on self-love or self-interest, but he thinks that benevolence is a limited phenomenon.
  B. He thought that altruism, while a real phenomenon in many areas of life, is not a motive that we can depend on in market activity, because much of it occurs among people who have no altruistic attachment to one another.
  C. His example of universal opulence is the woolen coat worn by common day laborers in Britain. He shows that the number of people involved in making this coat is enormous.

V. The model begins with self-interest as the motive of human interaction in the marketplace, and the main form of that interaction is exchange.
  A. Exchange makes possible the division of labor, which was the great mechanism that increased human productivity. He illustrates its advantages by describing a pin-making factory.
  B. Smith attributed the tremendous expansion of productivity to the division of labor through specialization, which led to greater skills and saved time, and new inventions that reduced the amount of required labor.
  C. So self-interest leads to market exchange, which makes possible the division of labor and the growth in human productivity, which mean more things can be produced more cheaply.
  D. The wider the market, and the more people who are involved in it, the more effective will be the productive effects of the division of labor.

VI. A second model explained the conditions under which goods would be sold at the lowest price possible.
  A. Each good sold in the marketplace had what Smith termed the "natural price." This was the lowest price at which it could continue to be produced.
  B. The price at which a commodity was sold had to reflect the average cost of labor, the average profits to be gained by investing money, and the average rent paid to landlords for using their land.

- C. Smith calls the actual price at which a commodity was sold the "market price."
- D. The market price is determined by the relationship between supply and effective demand.
- E. Smith explained how under conditions of market competition, the market price would tend toward the natural price.
- F. The market, therefore, was the most efficient institutional mechanism by which to channel self-interest toward the wealth of the nation.

VII. Smith, as a social scientist, could explain the logic that transformed the quest for self-interest into universal opulence, which brings us to Smith's "invisible hand."
- A. He explained how individuals who pursue their self-interest through the competitive market are compelled into actions that ultimately have beneficial social effects.
- B. Without intending to promote the public interest, they are compelled to do so by the structure of incentives offered by the market.
- C. This image of the invisible hand is a metaphor for the socially positive, unintended consequences of the institution of the market, which through increasing productivity and declining prices, channels the self-interest of individuals into collective benefits.

Suggested Reading:

Smith, *The Wealth of Nations*, especially Book I, chaps. 1–3 (division of labor), 7–8 (natural price and market price); Book IV, chap. 2 (the invisible hand).

Muller, *Adam Smith in His Time and Ours*, chaps. 1–6.

Evensky, *Adam Smith's Moral Philosophy*.

Questions to Consider:
1. Is there anything mysterious about the "invisible hand"?
2. Why do so many people find the notion that self-interested behavior can have socially beneficial outcomes disturbing?

Lecture Seven—Transcript
Seeing the Invisible Hand—Adam Smith

Adam Smith is one of those names in intellectual history about which many people think they know something. But what they think they know isn't always quite right. Perhaps they've met someone wearing an Adam Smith tie, who has told them about the wonders of self-interest. Perhaps they've heard the phrase the "invisible hand," which many people regard as a kind of magical mystery that makes the market work.

Some people have heard that Adam Smith was a great defender of capitalism, which leads them to assume that he's a great defender of capitalists. And some think they know that he was opposed to government, or as it's known in some circles, to government intervention.

Adam Smith did, indeed, write about self-interest, but without regarding it as automatically beneficial or as the last word in the explanation of human behavior. He did use the term "invisible hand," which turns out to be a great metaphor for a process that is in no sense mysterious. And as for his views on capitalists and on government, well, wait and see.

In this lecture, we'll look briefly at who Adam Smith was and at some of the key historical experiences that formed the backdrop of his writings on the market, especially the process that historians call the "consumer revolution" of 18th-century Britain. And we'll then explore some of the key contentions of his book, *The Wealth of Nations*, about how markets worked and how they could be made to work better, how they could be made to provide a higher standard of living to the vast majority of the population.

We'll look at Smith's contentions about how self-interest can be channeled to socially beneficial effects. We'll look at his explanation of how human productivity can be increased in ways that make it possible to produce ever more goods, and we'll explore his notion of how a competitive market can make those goods available to more and more people, lifting them out of material want into greater material comfort.

Adam Smith's *Inquiry into the Nature and Causes of the Wealth of Nations*, to call his most famous book by its full title, emerged out of Smith's reflections upon the real successes of 18th-century Britain in producing economic growth. Smith began with experience, with an analysis of existing institutions. He asked why they worked, what prevented them from working better, and he made recommendations for how they could be reformed to work better yet.

By profession, Adam Smith was a Professor of Philosophy at a time when philosophy included much of what we now call the social sciences. Smith was born in Kirkcaldy, a small town on the east coast of Scotland, in 1723. He was an exceptional student. He was sent to study at the University of Glasgow and then at Oxford on scholarship. His peers recognized his brilliance, and at the age of 27, he was appointed to a Professorship of Philosophy.

His first book, *The Theory of Moral Sentiments*, was published in 1759. It's a remarkable work, as remarkable in its own way as *The Wealth of Nations*. In it, Adam Smith sets out a social scientific explanation of how people become moral beings. His answer is too complex for us to explore here, but it's worth remarking upon the very first sentence of *The Theory of Moral Sentiments*. There he asserts that:

> No matter how selfish we suppose man to be, there is obviously something in his nature that makes him interested in the fortunes of others and makes their happiness necessary to him, even if he derives nothing from it other than the pleasure of seeing it.

In other words, though Adam Smith would later write a great deal about the role of self-interest in human affairs, he regarded the attempt to explain all of human action on the basis of self-interest or self-love as patently absurd.

One of the most important developments in 18th-century European life, as we've seen, was the increasing role of commerce. More and more of production was not for one's own consumption but in order to sell to others, to earn money with which to buy goods in the marketplace. And nowhere was this commercialization more evident than in the case of Smith's own Scotland. Not long before Smith was born, Scotland had entered into a political union with England, and an economic union as well. That meant that the Scots could now sell freely into England, and they became part of a much larger British economy. That acted as an economic stimulus and led the largely agricultural economy of Scotland to a more market-oriented form of agriculture, and a more productive one, so that Scotland regularly produced more grain than it consumed, making famine a historical memory by Smith's time.

Scotland was being transformed by the country's absorption into the larger economy of Britain, which included the international economy of the British Empire. Indeed, Glasgow, where Smith lived for a number of years, grew as a port to which tobacco was shipped from the New World to then be transshipped to elsewhere in England and then to the Continent.

Across Europe, philosophers and men of letters in the 18th century were turning their attention to the spread of commerce and reflecting on its moral and political implications. We've seen that Jean-Jacques Rousseau, who was critical of what passed for progress, wrote in his "Discourse on Inequality" of 1755 that in a commercial society, "the privileged few gorge themselves with luxuries, while the starving multitude lack the bare necessities of life." Once Smith finished *The Theory of Moral Sentiments*, he also turned his attention to reflecting on the implications of the growth of commerce. He started to lecture on political economy to his students at Edinburgh, but with conclusions that were very different from Rousseau's.

Smith was lured away from his university post by a rich nobleman who hired the professor to tutor the nobleman's son, and to accompany him on the grand tour; that is, on a trip to continental Europe, as Hobbes had done a century before with the Cavendish family. And there, in continental Europe, Smith discussed his developing ideas about the economy with many of the leading figures of the French Enlightenment and with French policymakers.

As part of his compensation package for taking on this role of tutor, Smith was granted a pension when the trip was over, a pension that allowed him to pursue his research and writing without interruption. So he moved to London, where he read, socialized with other intellectuals, and consulted with merchants and politicians, people who increasingly turned to him for advice on government economic policy.

After publishing *The Wealth of Nations* in 1776, Smith took up a post as commissioner of customs for Scotland; that is to say, Adam Smith lived out his days after finishing *The Wealth of Nations* as a government official, a reminder that government was by no means a stigmatized institution for Adam Smith.

The Wealth of Nations was written against the background of what historians now call the "consumer revolution." Most people in the Great Britain of Smith's day lived in what most of us would regard as poverty—poverty, like luxury, being a relative notion. And yet the population of Britain was probably better off economically than that of any other major nation on the globe, with the possible exception of the Dutch.

Economic conditions in his time were improving slowly, but demonstrably. The nation was becoming wealthier, not only its elite, but its laboring masses as well. Perhaps for the first time in history there was a near universal expectation of acquiring a basic minimum of food and shelter and clothing, and contemporary observers were struck by the relative ease with which an ordinary laborer could provide the means of subsistence for himself and for his family. In fact, when we look at the fortunes of the great 18th-century entrepreneurs in England, we see that they were made by entrepreneurs who owned companies that were cheaply producing goods that could appeal to a mass market: pots, candlesticks, cutlery, crockery, sauce pans. And then there were objects that had long been reserved for the rich but increasingly came within the reach of a larger part of society. A river of new consumer goods flowed into British homes: new blankets, linens, pillows, rugs, curtains, kitchenware made from pewter and glass and china and brass and copper. And this flow of new affordable goods, together with improvements in marketing and sales, formed what we now call the consumer revolution of 18th-century Britain.

Some of these goods came up from abroad, but not very many, because in Smith's day most policymakers viewed trade with other European powers as a form of undeclared warfare, with the object of maximizing benefits to England while minimizing those to rival nations. And the prime weapons in this war were prohibitions on the import of goods, or heavy government duties on imported goods that made them less profitable to bring into the country.

The Wealth of Nations was a book written about the market by a moral philosopher and public-policy advisor who had turned his mind to commerce with the aim of providing policies that would promote the well-being of the great majority of the populace. It wasn't a book written for merchants or manufacturers or investors. It doesn't offer advice on how individuals can get rich. It does offer advice on how nations as a whole can get wealthier. And by the nation, Smith meant not its elites but the common people. The goal of Smith's analysis was to bring about what he called "universal opulence," or what we would now call "mass affluence." By that, Smith meant a respectable standard of living for as many people as possible, a standard of living that would be possible if more and more people were able to afford to buy goods in the commercial marketplace.

The rise in the standard of living had been growing in 18th-century Britain, even for the working poor. But in Smith's eyes, economic growth was hampered by existing protectionist restrictions, so much of *The Wealth of Nations* was an argument for expanding the freedom to trade both within Britain and to the realm of international commerce.

The Wealth of Nations was a work of political economy, and political economy, according to Smith, had two objectives. The first was to provide plentiful subsistence to the people. *The Wealth of Nations* is divided up into five books, and that's the subject of the first four books of *The Wealth of Nations*. Their grand theme is how institutions can be structured to provide the cheapest and most plentiful supply of goods to consumers.

The second objective of political economy, as Smith conceived of it, was to provide the state with sufficient revenue to cover the cost of public services, and so the fifth and last book of *The Wealth of Nations* deals with the necessary roles of government and how government can best raise the revenue necessary for those goals.

Let's turn now to the crux of Smith's argument. Smith lays out what we would now call a "model" of the capitalist economy, actually a couple of key models. By "models," we mean a simplified, abstract explanation of some aspect of reality. His model of the commercial economy was based on observation, and then on generalization from those observations. Smith had a talent for creating these models, that is, for making useful generalizations that allow us to get a conceptual handle on the messy complex reality around us. He also had a knack for providing examples to help us see the point of the models that he was laying out.

In a few pithy sentences near the beginning of *The Wealth of Nations*, Smith sets out the first element of his model, and that is self-interest as a motivating force in market activity. As he famously put it:

> It is not from the benevolence of the butcher, the brewer, or the baker, that we expect our dinner, but from their regard to their own interest. We address ourselves, not to their humanity but to their self-love, and never talk to them of our own necessities but of their advantages.

Now, notice that contrary to the stereotypes about Adam Smith's thought, Smith is not claiming that all of human relations are based on self-love or self-interest. Remember that he says in the beginning of *The Theory of Moral Sentiments* that that's demonstrably not the case, but he thinks that what he called "benevolence," or what we would probably call "altruism," is a limited phenomenon. Most people, he thinks, are altruistic to one degree or another, but their altruism is usually most intense toward those who they know and who they care about. But the market is about exchanges between people who by and large don't know one another. As we'll see, it's about exchanges between people who have often never met, and who don't even know that the people on whom they depend for their purchases even exist. So altruism, while a real phenomenon in many areas of life, is not a motive that we can depend on in market activity.

In a striking image, Smith gives us an example of what he calls universal opulence, that is to say, a situation in which most people are able to acquire the useful commodities they need through the market. He takes the case of a woolen coat worn by a common day laborer in Britain. That is to say, a common article that was now affordable by the great mass of the population thanks to the consumer revolution.

Smith points out that the number of people involved in making this woolen coat is enormous; that is to say, there are hundreds of people who have worked or provided their services in order for this common laborer to wear the coat that protects him from the cold. And Smith enumerates them. There's the shepherd, who raises the sheep. There's the sorter of wool. There are the people who comb the wool, the ones who dye the wool, the ones who spin the wool, the ones who clean the wool, who weave the wool into cloth, who sew the cloth into a coat. And then there are many merchants and carriers who are involved in transporting the materials from around the country. And the chemicals used to dye the cloth actually come from around the world.

Smith reminds us that to bring those substances to England, those dyes, required many shipbuilders, sailors, sail makers. All of these people, then, have contributed to making it possible for the day laborer to have his coat—people who the day laborer doesn't know, or even suspect exist. No wonder he can't depend on their altruism to get his coat. And yet, get a coat he does, and at a price that even he can afford. How is that possible?

That's what Adam Smith sets out to explain in his model of how self-interest can lead to this sort of universal opulence. The model, then, begins with self-interest as the mode of human interaction in the marketplace. And the main form of that interaction is exchange. You give me something that you have and that I want, for something that I have and that you want. That something that we exchange may be our labor. It may be the use of land. It may be a commodity like wool or a coat. And, of course, it may be money, which can be used to pay for labor, or for land, or for any commodity. So self-interest leads to exchange.

The fact that we exchange makes possible the division of labor. Instead of making everything that I need for myself, I make or do one thing in particular. I grow apples, or I work in a factory, or I give lectures. I sell my labor or my apples or my lectures in the market and exchange the money for what I get for what I've sold to buy the other things that I want. This division of labor, Smith maintained, was the great mechanism that increased human productivity. And he illustrates its advantages by describing a pin-making factory, in which an assembly line of 10 persons, each specialized in a particular function, creates far more pins than if each of the pin makers had tried to make the pins all on their own.

One man, as he describes it, pulls out the metal wire. Another straightens it out. A third cuts it to the right size. A fourth creates a point at one end. Another 3 men make the head of the pin, and another joins the head of the pin to the shaft of the pin. Yet another person colors the pin, and another person places the pins into the paper into which they are to be shipped. Together, as Smith describes it, 10 men working in this fashion were able to produce 48,000 pins per day. Had they been working as individuals, each making the pins on his own, the 10 men might each produce 20 pins each a day at most, for a total of 200 pins. So the division of labor in this case had increased production by 240 times.

Now, in using the pin factory to make his point, Smith was not touting the advantages of the factory form of production, that is to say, in which the entire production process took place under one roof. The factory was merely the form in which the division of labor was most immediately visible; that is to say, it was easy to picture. It was easy to comprehend. That made the pin factory useful for explaining the much larger social process in which the division of labor was spread over many sites in society as was the case, for example, with the woolen coat.

Smith attributed the tremendous expansion of productivity brought about by the division of labor to several factors. First of all, the division of labor was based on specialization, and that led workers to develop greater skill as they performed their specialized tasks. It also saved time that would otherwise be lost in switching from one task to another. And, he thought, it favored the invention of new devices that cut down on the amount of work required.

So, here's the model again so far. Self-interest leads to market exchange. Exchange makes possible the division of labor and the growth in human productivity, and that makes it possible, eventually, for more things to be produced more cheaply. And the wider the market, the more people who are involved in it, the more effective will be the productive effects of the division of labor.

But how could the market provide goods at prices that more and more people could afford to purchase? Sure, they were being made more and more inexpensively because of the division of labor through the market, but how could common people afford them? Well, here Smith lays out a second model that explained the conditions under which goods would be sold at the lowest price possible.

Here's his reasoning. He says that for each commodity—that is to say, for every good that is sold in the marketplace at any given time—there was what he terms the "natural price." The natural price was the lowest price at which some good could continue to be produced. Smith reasons that the price at which a commodity was sold, this natural price, had to reflect the average cost of labor in society, the average profits to be gained by investing money, and the average rent paid to landlords for using their land. So the natural price was the lowest price at which that commodity could be produced without laborers or entrepreneurs or landlords losing money and, hence, taking their land or their labor or their money elsewhere.

Now this natural price, you'll notice, represents the price that's most beneficial to consumers. It's the lowest price at which the commodity can continue to be made. And in a commercial society, all men and women were consumers, whatever else they might be. Consumers want goods to be available as cheaply as possible so that they can afford the goods that are being produced. So on the one hand, then, we have this model of the natural price, the lowest price at which a good can continue to be produced.

The actual price at which a commodity was sold Smith calls the "market price." The market price of the commodity was determined by the relationship between the quantity of goods supplied by producers of that commodity and the amount of that commodity that was demanded by those with an ability to pay for it, that is to say, what Smith calls "effective demand."

I might, in theory, want to buy a Jaguar, but given the other things that I want to buy with my salary, I may not want to devote enough of my salary to buying a Jaguar, therefore, I don't provide effective demand for it. Effective demand is those things that we want and that we're willing to pay for and have the ability to pay for.

So the market price is determined by the relationship between supply and effective demand. And now Smith explained why the market price of commodities would tend toward the natural price, the price, you'll recall, that's best for consumers. And he also explained how the supply of these goods would tend toward the level of demand, and all of this without anyone in a position of authority deciding on the amount that should be produced or the price at which those things should be sold.

At any given moment, he reasoned, the market price could be above the natural price or below the natural price. If the market price goes below the natural price, then those who produce the commodity would be motivated by self-interest to produce some other commodity where they could make a larger profit, and that would lead to a decreased supply of that original commodity. And once the supply went down, the market price would rise again.

If the market price of a commodity went above the natural price, then those people who had capital or labor would be attracted to move their resources toward producing that commodity since it provided a higher than average profit or a higher than average wage. In time, therefore, the supply of the commodity would go up and its market price would go down, making that commodity more available to consumers.

The moral of Smith's analysis was that when the market was structured to operate along the lines of his models, market prices would tend to provide more and more goods at the cheapest prices at which they could be produced. In this sense, the market would provide the greatest possible benefit to consumers. The market, therefore, was the most efficient institutional mechanism by which to channel self-interest toward the wealth of the nation, and especially to promote the well-being of the bulk of its citizens by providing them with more goods at prices that more and more people could afford.

You will notice that none of those involved in the production of commodities were primarily motivated to provide their services by a concern for the welfare of the consumer: not the laborers who provided their labor, not the landlords who provided their land, not the entrepreneurs who invested their capital. Each of these people pursued their self-interest, but by pursuing their self-interest through the market, they ended up benefiting consumers.

Smith, as a social scientist, could explain the logic that transformed the quest for self-interest into universal opulence. Once the logic of the market mechanism was understood, it could more easily be put into place by policymakers, who were now in a position to anticipate the positive social effects of the market mechanism.

That brings us to Smith's famous image of the "invisible hand." He's explained how individuals who pursue their self-interest through the competitive market are compelled into actions that ultimately have beneficial social effects. Without intending to promote the public interest, they end up doing so, and they're compelled to do so by the structure of incentives offered by the market.

In a famous metaphor, Smith writes that while the individual "intends only his own gain ... he is ... led by an invisible hand to promote an end which was no part of his intention." This image of the invisible hand is a metaphor for the socially positive, unintended consequences of the institution of the market, which through increasing productivity and declining prices, channels the self-interest of individuals into collective benefits.

There is nothing mysterious about the invisible hand, at least once its functions have been explained by Smith's social scientific explanation. And yet, because of the gap between the explicit intentions of the actors in the market and the ultimate results of their action, the notion that the social outcome of the market process is socially beneficial is counterintuitive. The consumer knows from his experience that the merchant sells him a commodity for more than the merchant paid for it. Not only that, but after having tried to purchase it as cheaply as possible, the merchant tries to sell it for the most that he can get. Most consumers would be at a loss to explain how they benefit from a system made up of many such merchants, but Smith does explain it, which is why *The Wealth of Nations* remains the starting point for understanding a capitalist economy. And that's why some version of Smith's analysis is now found in every economics textbook.

What such textbooks tend to leave out is Smith's exploration of why real life so often diverges from his model, and that is the topic of our next lecture.

Lecture Eight
Smith on Merchants, Politicians, Workers

Scope:

Adam Smith argued that free international trade would expand the economic benefits of the market. It would also have the political benefit of diminishing conflict between nations through mutually beneficial trade. Much of *The Wealth of Nations* is devoted to showing how the reality of contemporary capitalism diverged from the desirable, competitive model that Smith had set out. By a variety of means, including the lobbying of politicians, each economic group tries to avoid the competitive market. Each group tries to promote its self-interest at the expense of the general interest. The role of intellectuals, for Smith, is to combat these pressures and urge policymakers to promote competitive markets that serve the general interest, in order to attain "universal opulence."

Outline

I. Many people mistakenly believe that Adam Smith asserted that everything would work out for the best if people merely followed their self-interests.
   A. This argument that self-interest can have socially beneficial outcomes has a kind of repulsion for some people and an attraction to others for that very reason.
   B. Smith's analysis was far more subtle, and we'll take into consideration his major works: *The Wealth of Nations*, *The Theory of Moral Sentiments*, and the *Lectures on Jurisprudence*.

II. Self-interest actually plays a pernicious role in economic matters in *The Wealth of Nations*.
   A. From the point of view of the public interest, it was most beneficial for people to pursue their self-interest by channeling it through the market, but from the point of view of the producer it was most beneficial to circumvent the competitive market.

B. The market would produce the best possible outcome for consumers under the conditions Smith called "free competition," but as Smith showed, much of European society and government was still structured to prevent free competition.

III. Smith thought that the proper task of the legislator concerned with the public interest was to prevent the short-circuiting of the market mechanism despite organized economic interests seeking to protect themselves from market competition.

A. Smith showed that wherever and whenever individuals or groups could promote their own interests at the expense of the public by bypassing the free market, they would. *The Wealth of Nations* is a great compendium of such attempts.

B. Market competition creates difficulty in making profits. And from the point of view of those producing goods and services, free competition, or market competition, also makes you work harder.

C. Smith showed that the citizens of the towns contrived with one another to keep up the price of urban-made goods at the expense of the people in the countryside.

D. He noted that merchants, whenever they have the opportunity to get together, will try to conspire to pursue their self-interests. When they did so in ways that went around the market, then it redounded to their benefit at the expense of the larger public.

E. Both workers and employers also tried to organize to circumvent the market for labor, but under contemporary conditions the law and the nature of political influence in an undemocratic parliamentary system favored the employers.

F. The most effective means of circumventing the competition of the market was through legal monopolies that gave an individual or a trading company the sole right to sell a particular product.

IV. For Smith, most of the existing regulation of foreign commerce was motivated by one or another group of merchants or manufacturers trying to limit competition for their goods.
  A. The favorite method of eliminating competition at the time was by prohibiting foreign imports or placing heavy duties on them.
  B. Smith showed that these measures were inimical to the public interest because they raised the price of goods to consumers.
  C. Most of Book IV of *The Wealth of Nations* is devoted to an attack on the policies of international trade based on a view of international economic relations as a zero-sum game in which one nation's gain must be another's loss.
  D. The model of international relations that Smith sets out in *The Wealth of Nations* is a model of economic and political relations along more cosmopolitan and more peaceful lines.

V. One function of public-spirited intellectuals like himself, as Smith understood it, was to counteract national prejudices and the zero-sum conception of economic life that led to international conflict.
  A. Smith coined the term "mercantile system" to describe the dominant economic doctrine because he believed that it reflected both the interests and the mentality of merchants and manufacturers, whose quest for monopoly had been extended into a view of international commerce.
  B. This notion of the advantages of international trade was reconceptualized and expanded a generation later by David Ricardo, who coined the term "comparative advantage."
  C. According to Smith, the prosperity of other nations was based on the fact that they produced things that the British wanted to buy—and those other countries, as they became more prosperous, provided a market for the goods and services that the British could produce most efficiently.
  D. One of the main notions that he wanted to convey in *The Wealth of Nations* is that nations benefit when other nations are rich and productive, are a source of goods, and provide a market as well.

VI. Smith showed that the pursuit of self-interest does not automatically or inevitably lead to the public benefit. But how can one keep individuals and groups from trying to use their political influence to benefit themselves at the expense of the public?

- **A.** One of the purposes of *The Wealth of Nations* was to warn politicians and policymakers of the dangers that protective legislation and other ways of getting around the market posed to the development of most of the populace.
- **B.** Smith wrote the book in good part to counter what he termed the "sophistry and clamour" of individuals and groups urging legislation that would protect them from market competition.
- **C.** In the Britain of Smith's day, the right to vote was confined to a wealthy few; only their "sophistry and clamour" counted.
- **D.** Since Smith's day, the right to vote has become more universal. That doesn't mean that the problem has gone away; it has simply become more widespread.

Suggested Reading:

Smith, *The Wealth of Nations*, Book IV, chaps. 1–8.

Muller, *Adam Smith in His Time and Ours*, chap. 5.

Questions to Consider:

1. Has the balance of power between employers and employees changed since Smith's day? If so, why, in what direction, and does it make the problems he addressed more or less pressing?
2. Smith lamented in his day that

> Each nation has been made to look with an invidious eye upon the prosperity of all the nations with which it trades, and to consider their gain as its own loss. Commerce, which ought naturally to be, among nations as among individuals, a bond of union and friendship, has become the most fertile source of discord and animosity.

How relevant is Smith's lament today?

Lecture Eight—Transcript
Smith on Merchants, Politicians, Workers

Smith's key insight in *The Wealth of Nations* about the way in which self-interest can lead to benevolent outcomes in which individuals pursuing their self-interest can have socially beneficial effects—that idea is so striking it seems to illuminate so many elements of economic reality, and so many elements, perhaps, of reality in general, that some people are struck by it and actually blinded by it; that is to say, they take Smith to assert that self-interest always has beneficial effects, and that was not his contention.

This argument that self-interest can have socially beneficial outcomes has a kind of repulsion for some people and an attraction to others for that very reason. The repulsion comes from the counterintuitive nature of the argument, the fact that there is a gap between our intentions and our outcomes. That often makes moralists uncomfortable to the extent to which people think of moral action as based on intention rather than on outcomes. The fact that self-interest can have a socially beneficial outcome is disturbing to moralists who want to see a kind of direct relationship between intention and outcome.

Conversely, because Smith has shown the gap between intentions and outcome, the fact that self-interest can have collective benefits, it has a kind of ironic quality to it. And that, in the minds of some people, makes it all the more attractive, the fact that they now have some insight into reality, thanks to Adam Smith, that seems to explain so much of reality and that not everybody else has. So the kind of counterintuitive or ironic nature actually makes the argument about the potentially beneficial effects of self-interest even more attractive to some of Smith's readers. And so they, too, mistakenly assume that Smith asserted that everything would work out for the best if people merely followed their self-interest.

In fact, as we'll see, Adam Smith's analysis was far more subtle, and in this lecture and the next couple on Adam Smith, I want to take into consideration *The Wealth of Nations* and sometimes round out the insights in *The Wealth of Nations* with statements of Smith's from his other major published work, *The Theory of Moral Sentiments*, which is a book that he wrote before *The Wealth of Nations* and then revised after finishing *The Wealth of Nations*. So it's not like he changed his mind after *The Wealth of Nations*. And sometimes I'll want to take quotations from what we know now as the *Lectures on Jurisprudence*.

Adam Smith's intention, when he was a professor, was to write a book on the basis of morality, that is, *The Theory of Moral Sentiments*; to write another book on political economy that became *The Wealth of Nations*; and he wanted to write another book about political and legal institutions. He never got around to finishing that book, and in an action that is very frustrating for intellectual historians and other admirers of Smith's work, he instructed those who were in charge of his estate, on his deathbed, to take the manuscript of this unfinished book on politics and throw it into the fire in front of his eyes, which they did. Which might lead you to think that we have no idea of what Smith's views were on larger political and jurisprudential issues, but in fact, a couple of students who had been his students at the University of Glasgow took notes on Smith's lectures, and those notes were discovered later in the 19th century—and in the 20th century have been published as his *Lectures on Jurisprudence*. So some of the insights in *The Wealth of Nations* are rounded out by taking into consideration *The Theory of Moral Sentiments* and Smith's *Lectures on Jurisprudence*, and sometimes Smith's correspondence helps to round them out, too.

Smith's analysis of self-interest was far more subtle and complex than the notion that self-interest always has beneficial outcomes. We've seen that Smith had already insisted in *The Theory of Moral Sentiments* that the notion that you could explain all human actions on the basis of self-interest was at odds with our experience. But self-interest can also play, and does also play, a pernicious role in economic matters in *The Wealth of Nations*, and that's what I want to explore today.

Smith showed, of course, in *The Wealth of Nations* that from the point of view of the public interest, it was most beneficial for every person to pursue their self-interest by channeling it through the market. That's from the point of view of the public interest. But from the point of view of the individual producer or a group of producers, it was most beneficial to circumvent the competitive market, to get around it, to get around and avoid market competition.

Smith said in *The Wealth of Nations* that the market would produce the best possible outcome for consumers under conditions of what he called "free competition"—that is to say, a situation where there was free sale of land, where it wasn't restricted on the basis of who the owner was; where there was relatively easy entry for new merchants into existing markets; and where there were few restrictions on the hiring of labor. But as he showed in *The Wealth of Nations*, much of European society and government was still structured to prevent free competition, and—and this is the important point about self-interest—that was no accident, Smith thought. It was because the self-interest of individuals or of groups of producers was in fact often at odds with the public interest. And because of that, the proper task of the legislator who tried to concern himself with the public interest was to prevent individuals and groups of people from short-circuiting the market mechanism, and to prevent them from doing that despite the fact that there would be organized economic interests trying to protect themselves from market competition.

Smith shows that wherever and whenever individuals or groups could promote their own interests at the expense of the public interest by bypassing the free market, they would. And *The Wealth of Nations* is in many ways a great compendium of such attempts. They would try to do so because the free market, market competition, is tough. First of all, market competition creates difficulty in making profits. The more competition, the more difficult it is to make profits. That's why people want to avoid it if they can.

From the point of view of those producing goods and services, free competition, market competition, also makes you work harder. It's easier if you can prevent competition, and then perhaps you can work less hard than your now nonexistent competitor. So people had self-interested motives for trying to get around the market, and *The Wealth of Nations*, then, is a great assemblage and demonstration of all the ways in which individuals and groups of producers try to get around the free market.

Smith showed that the citizens of the towns contrived with one another to keep up the price of urban-made goods at the expense of the people in the countryside. He showed that there were legal privileges still held by guilds that restricted the supply of labor into specific occupations, and that, therefore, helped keep wages above the market price. And that also restricted the supply of commodities, thus keeping profits above the natural price, that price that was best for consumers.

As for merchants, Smith writes in one of the more famous passages of *The Wealth of Nations* that "people of the same trade seldom meet together, even for merriment and diversion, but the conversation ends in a conspiracy against the publick, or in some contrivance to raise prices." That's the quote, and you'll notice the notion here that merchants, whenever they have the opportunity to get together, will try to conspire either to limit the price of labor; or to divide the market among themselves so that there won't be market competition; or to collude on pricing, saying that they won't compete against one another in terms of lower prices, that they'll maintain some price; and so on. Smith thought, again, this was not because merchants were particularly evil. They were no different from everyone else. They were merely pursuing their self-interests, and when they did so in ways that went around the market, then it redounded to their benefit at the expense of the larger public.

Smith shows that both workers and employers try to circumvent the free market for labor. The workers try to raise their wages beyond what free competition would allow by associating together and saying that they wouldn't work for any less. The employers try to lower the wages that were paid to labor by agreeing among themselves only to pay a certain low wage. Both groups, Smith shows, try to organize for this self-interested purpose. But under contemporary conditions—that is, under the conditions of the late 18th century—the contest was unequal, first of all because the law prohibited workers from combining in order to raise the price of their labor. But it didn't prohibit employers from combining to try to keep wages down.

The employers also had another advantage, and that was their superior political influence. As Smith writes, "Whenever the legislature attempts to regulate the differences between masters and their workmen, its counselors are always the masters." That was because of the difference in political power between the employers, the people that Smith refers to as "masters," and their workmen. By and large, the masters had the vote. They could vote for members of Parliament, and under the very limited suffrage of the time, most workmen didn't have the vote.

Smith points out that under the circumstances of the time, employers also had other advantages. In case of a strike, they could usually hold out longer than workers because those workers often depended on wages for their daily sustenance. And because employers were fewer in number, it was easier for them to connive without calling attention to themselves. The most effective means of circumventing the competition of the market was through legal monopolies that gave an individual or a trading company the sole right to sell a particular product.

For Smith, most of the existing regulation of foreign commerce in Britain was motivated by one or another group of merchants or manufacturers who were trying to limit competition for the goods that they made or sold. Smith pointed out that these merchants and manufacturers had a lot of political weight. They were well placed to exercise political influence, first of all because they were located in cities, especially London, which of course is where Parliament was.

Secondly, no less importantly, they had money and favors with which to influence politicians. Smith also points out that they had their own articulate spokesmen; that is to say, they hired writers who presented the interests of particular groups of merchants and manufacturers as if it was in the public interest. And what these writers typically did was try to explain that it was in the national interest to prevent competition in this or that branch of commerce for which they were hired to defend.

The favorite method of eliminating competition at the time was by prohibiting foreign imports or by placing heavy duties on them that made it economically unprofitable to bring them into the country. There were, for example, prohibitions enacted in 1721 against the importation of calicoes, a popular kind of cotton at the time. In 1748, the wearing of French linens was prohibited. From 1763 to 1776, so in those very years in which Smith was writing *The Wealth of Nations*, there was a new spate of legislation that prohibited the importation of all sorts of things, of foreign silk and leather gloves and stockings and velvet. And there was an increase in duties on some other commodities, on linen and on various types of paper. And Smith argued that these measures were inimical to the public interest because they raised the price of goods to consumers.

So, most of Book IV of *The Wealth of Nations* is devoted to an attack on the policies of international trade that were dominant in Europe at the time. Those policies were based on a view of international economic relations as a zero-sum game—that is, a situation in which one nation's gain had to be another's loss. International trade was largely perceived as a tacit war against rival nations, and this tacit struggle, as we've seen, often led to actual military confrontations in an attempt to secure trade privileges or trade routes or colonies.

One of the most important elements of *The Wealth of Nations* was that the book provided a counter model of international relations to this conception of international relations as a zero-sum game and as a kind of tacit war where one had to lose in order for the other one to gain.

The model of international relations that Smith sets out in *The Wealth of Nations* is a model of economic and political relations along more cosmopolitan and more peaceful lines. You could say that the worldview behind Smith's ideas about this is actually most clearly expressed in his *Theory of Moral Sentiments*. Here's the way he puts it. He says the growing prosperity of other nations

> are all proper objects of our national emulation, not of national prejudice or envy. Mankind are benefited, human nature is ennobled by them. In such improvements each nation ought not only to endeavor itself to excel, but, from the love of mankind, to promote, instead of obstructing, the excellence of its neighbours.

So this was supposed to provide a more cosmopolitan view; a view that saw the well-being of others, of those in other nations, as conducive to our own well-being instead of at odds with or in competition with our own well-being. One function of public-spirited intellectuals like himself, as Smith understood it, was to counteract national prejudices that said we ought to be concerned only about ourselves, and to counteract this zero-sum conception of economic life that led to international conflict.

One finds this nationalist notion, of course, today. We find writers, television commentators, or politicians who speak as if the economic success of other nations should be somehow regarded as a threat to our own well-being. So the sentiments that Smith was trying to combat in the 18th century continue.

Smith described this dominant economic doctrine as the "mercantile system." That's a term that he actually coined. People sometimes think that this term the "mercantile system," or "mercantilism," was used in the 17th and 18th centuries by its proponents. It wasn't. It was a term coined by Smith, who was an opponent of those policies because he believed that those policies reflected both the interests and the mentality of merchants.

It wasn't merchants and their supporters who used the term "mercantilism," just as later on it wasn't capitalists who first used the term "capitalism." As we've seen, it was coined by Marx to stigmatize the phenomenon it was describing. That's what Smith was doing in calling this system of prohibitions the mercantile system.

As Smith saw it, the quest of these merchants and manufacturers had been to extend this notion of monopoly into international commerce and to present the view that taught that each nation's interest, as he put it, "consisted in beggaring all their neighbours."

Why did Smith refer to this as the mercantile system? You'll notice there is some truth to his notion that this is the extension into international relations of a view of the world that is common among merchants. If merchants are in direct competition for a limited market, then it's true that one merchant's gain of market share is at the expense of the other. In other words, to the extent that economic reality is a fixed pie, then if one gains, the other loses. But of course, that premise isn't true if the pie is growing, and in this case, the pie that Smith had in mind was the total of goods and services that were available internationally. Smith tried to show that the total amount could be made to grow through international trade. In that sense, there would be, or could be, more for everyone.

Smith's argument in favor of free international trade, of doing away with these prohibitions on the importation of goods, was that just as within a nation, a larger market made possible a greater division of labor, and a greater division of labor made possible greater productivity and hence, eventually, lower prices to consumers. So free international trade would create a larger market among nations, and his argument was that that would allow each nation to specialize in making the things that it could do most efficiently. He said it's possible to grow oranges in Paris, but it's very expensive. You need to grow them in an orangerie, in a greenhouse under glass, and so on. It's much more efficient to import them from southern climes and to sell to people in those southern climes the things that the French are better and more efficient in making.

This notion of the advantages of international trade was reconceptualized and expanded a generation later by David Ricardo, a famous British economist who, by the way, was the descendant of one of those Jewish families of Spanish origin who had made their way north after the expulsion from Spain, hence his Spanish-sounding last name.

Ricardo coined the term "comparative advantage," the notion that even if one country could make everything more efficiently and cheaply than a second country, it was still to the advantage of the first country to specialize in the things that it made best and to buy from a second country the things that *it* made most efficiently, and that there would be mutual gains from trade even in that kind of circumstance.

So as Smith maintained, the prosperity of other nations with which the British traded shouldn't be viewed as a threat. The prosperity of other nations was based on the fact that they produced things that the British wanted to buy. And those other countries, he argued, as they became more prosperous, provided a market for the goods and services that the British could produce most efficiently. In that sense this merchant's mentality that the gain of one is a loss for another was inappropriate and, indeed, counterproductive. Here's the way he put it:

> Each nation has been made to look with an invidious eye upon the prosperity of all the nations with which it trades, and to consider their gain as its own loss. Commerce, which ought naturally to be, among nations as among individuals, a bond of union and friendship, has become the most fertile source of discord and animosity.

So this was the view behind Smith's critique of contemporary mercantile policies in *The Wealth of Nations*, the notion that trade between nations, as in the case of trade between individuals and trade between groups, ought to be a source of concord, not of discord and animosity. And it became that kind of animosity that led to animosity when one assumed that trade was a zero-sum game.

That had occurred, according to Smith's analysis, because the trade policy of Europe had been led by what he called, "the interested sophistry of merchants and manufacturers." It had been led by that away from the recognition that "a nation that would enrich itself by foreign trade is certainly most likely to do so when its neighbours are all rich, industrious, and commercial nations." That is one of the main notions that he wanted to convey in *The Wealth of Nations*, that nations benefit when other nations are rich and productive, and are a source of goods, and provide a market as well.

So Smith showed that the pursuit of self-interest does not automatically or inevitably lead to the public benefit. But how can one keep individuals and groups from trying to use their political influence to benefit themselves at the expense of the public interest? How can one keep politicians from what you might call "taking the path of least resistance" and doing whatever their supporters from one or another organized economic lobby ask them to do?

The truth is that Smith had no definitive, knockdown answer to this dilemma, and some 20th-century economists (like the famous University of Chicago economist George Stigler) have criticized him for this, for the fact that he has a system that explains why people will pursue their self-interest, and they'll pursue it in politics as well, and he doesn't explain how to get around that—that is to say, how the public interest can be protected in a situation where so many individuals and so many groups are trying to use their political power to pressure politicians to adopt policies that will favor them by limiting the market and circumventing market competition.

It's true that Smith doesn't have an explicit argument about how to get out of this dilemma, but one of the purposes of *The Wealth of Nations* was to warn politicians and policymakers of the dangers that protective legislation and other ways of getting around the market posed to the development of the well-being of most of the populace. Smith wrote *The Wealth of Nations* in good part to counter what, in a letter written shortly after *The Wealth of Nations*, he termed the "sophistry and clamour," that is to say, the false knowledge being disseminated publicly by individuals and groups that were urging legislation that protected them from market competition.

In the Britain of Adam Smith's day, the vote was confined to a wealthy few; it was *their* sophistry and clamor that counted. Since Smith's day, in the course of the 19th and 20th centuries, the right to vote has become more universal, at least in modern democracies, but that doesn't mean that the problem that Smith had identified has gone away. It's simply become more widespread.

The problem, then, is that self-interest, when it's not properly channeled by the market, can be inimical to the public interest, where the public interest is understood as the free availability of more and more goods at lesser and lesser prices, leading to universal opulence. As we've seen, the channeling of self-interest to circumvent the market is not unnatural. You could say it's the way of the world. Rich individuals use their wealth to try to exert political power. So do whole industries. So do various professional associations. So do labor unions when they have the money or the votes with which to try to influence politicians.

So in Adam Smith's analysis, there is an ongoing tension within capitalist societies between the public interest that's best served when self-interest is channeled through the market in such a way that it leads to universal opulence, which requires a competitive market—there's a tension between that and the fact that individuals and groups in pursuit of their particular interests will do their best to get around market competition.

Self-interest is the great engine of economic growth and of the good things that economic growth can bring, but only if it's channeled properly because politicians, as we've seen, were subject in the 18th century (and still are) to the pressure of those with votes and money. And as Adam Smith conceived of it, the role of intellectuals like him was to keep an eye on the public interest, and in that sense, you see, Smith agreed with the civic republican tradition's conception of virtue, even if he didn't expect it from most people. He thought it was very essential for some people to have a sense of the public interest.

But the challenges to capitalist society, as Smith saw it, came not only from the ongoing difficulty of keeping the market as competitive as possible in order to benefit consumers. Smith thought that even when the capitalist market was functioning well, it created problems that posed a threat to national well-being.

In our next lecture, we'll look at those problems and Smith's solutions to them.

Lecture Nine
Smith on the Problems of Commercial Society

Scope:

Smith thought that a well-functioning government was a necessary prerequisite for a commercial society. Certain functions can only be provided by government, including national defense, the provision of law, and what we now call "infrastructure." Smith was also acutely aware that some of the very processes that made commercial society more productive, such as the division of labor, could have negative effects, which he thought it the duty of intellectuals like him to analyze and of government to alleviate.

Outline

I. Because Adam Smith's influence was probably greatest in providing arguments against direct government involvement in economic life, the crucial significance of government in his work is often overlooked.

   A. For Smith, the state was the most important institution on which modern commercial society depended.

   B. Smith believed that while the state ought to relinquish its direct economic role in enforcing tariffs, wage rates, and other restrictions on trade, the size and functions of the state would actually grow with the development of commercial society.

   C. The benefits of commercial society required a larger state, but the wealth generated by a well-functioning market economy would make the economic burden of the state bearable.

   D. This was stated most explicitly in his *Lectures on Jurisprudence*, and *The Wealth of Nations* devotes hundreds of pages to analyzing the proper functions of government and how to pay for them.

II. Smith's views on the functions of the modern state followed from his analysis of the anticipatable negative consequences of the central institutions of modern commercial society, namely, the market.
   A. If the spread of the market and the resulting intensification of the division of labor was the source or at least the precondition for much of what was best about modern civilized society, it was also the root of a number of intrinsic dangers.
   B. Smith thought that the role of intellectuals like him was to alert legislators to these dangers, with an eye toward obviating them.

III. One of those dangers dealt with the problem of national defense. The need for national defense grew more urgent with the progress of economic development.
   A. The record of history showed that as a society grew richer it became a more attractive object of attack by its poorer neighbors. At the same time, the division of labor created a style of life that left most men less fit to be soldiers.
   B. Smith provides a historical analysis of the development of institutions of defense, and he developed a model of historical stages of society, which was a way to show the connections between political, economic, military, and cultural developments.
   C. In the first three stages, wars didn't involve a great deal of additional expense to government, but at this time in history, war becomes more expensive for government.
   D. Smith believed that the art of war became more complex with the division of labor and that its mastery required the same specialization as did other fields.
   E. It was only the wise policy of the state that could attract some individuals to devote themselves fully to military matters, by the creation of a permanent army.
   F. Smith's acute historical awareness of the link between national defense and the preservation of civilization led him to insist on the primacy of defense over economic considerations in trade policy.

IV. Next to providing for the national defense against other sovereign states, the most important function of government was to provide justice and security under the law.
- **A.** It was only the state that protected property and hence made "private property" possible.
- **B.** Those with more property had a greater interest in maintaining the state, and they could enjoy their income only because of the protection offered by the state.
- **C.** It was on these grounds that he argued that the rich ought to be taxed at a higher rate than the poor.
- **D.** Another function of government that was bound to expand with the advance of commercial society was the provision of infrastructure.

V. In other words, *The Wealth of Nations* was much concerned with what in the language of modern economics are called "public goods."
- **A.** By providing for defense, justice, and infrastructure, government created the preconditions for a market economy.
- **B.** The role of government went further yet because it was up to the legislator to anticipate, and up to the intellectual to make the policymakers aware of, negative cultural effects so they could be mitigated and ameliorated.

VI. Smith argued that the very division of labor that increases human productivity has negative effects as well, especially upon manual workers.
- **A.** In a famous passage of *The Wealth of Nations*, he gives a really frightening portrait of the narrowing effects of the division of labor on the human psyche and the human soul.
- **B.** As an antidote to the mental degradation caused by the division of labor, Smith recommended the encouragement of universal public schooling, largely at government expense, so that even those in the lower ranks of society could acquire the essential skills of reading, writing, and arithmetic.
- **C.** The division of labor therefore not only stunted intellectual abilities by narrowing the horizons of the worker, it created economic incentives for the neglect of any formal education.

- **D.** In addition to the benefits of education for the individual, Smith thought, it was also a prime political consideration for the state to have a more educated populace to make political judgments as citizens.
- **VII.** Smith does maintain many elements of the civic republican tradition in a form more amenable to a commercial society.
  - **A.** The whole structure of *The Wealth of Nations* is intended to motivate policymakers toward the general interest.
  - **B.** Smith didn't think that every result of the market was good, nor did he think that every action of government was bad.

Suggested Reading:
Evensky, *Adam Smith's Moral Philosophy.*
Fleischacker, *On Adam Smith's "Wealth of Nations."*
Muller, *Adam Smith in His Time and Ours*, chaps. 6–13.
Smith, *The Wealth of Nations*, Book 5.

Questions to Consider:
1. Does providing for national defense remain a dilemma for contemporary capitalist societies?
2. Does Smith's description of the mentally stultifying effects of the division of labor have any contemporary relevance?

Lecture Nine—Transcript
Smith on the Problems of Commercial Society

Because Adam Smith's influence was probably greatest in providing arguments against direct government involvement in economic life, the crucial significance of government in his work is often overlooked. Smith did oppose much of the existing state economic regulation because he thought it reflected particular interests at the expense of the public interest. But for Smith, as for Hobbes, the state was the most important institution on which modern commercial society depended, and Smith believed that while the state ought to relinquish its direct economic role in things like enforcing tariffs or wage rates or other restrictions on trade, he thought that the size and functions of the state would actually grow with the development of commercial society.

He thought that the benefits of commercial society would require a larger state but that the wealth generated by a well-functioning market economy would make the economic burden of the state bearable. This is stated most explicitly in those *Lectures on Jurisprudence*, those lectures that Smith gave to his students that have come down to us in the form of student notes. Here's how Smith put it then. He said:

> We may observe that the government in a civilized country is much more expensive than in a barbarous one; and when we say that one government is more expensive than another, it is the same as if we said that the one country is farther advanced in improvement than [another]. ... There are many expenses necessary in a civilized country for which there is no occasion in [one] that is barbarous.

Given that assumption, it's not surprising that *The Wealth of Nations* devotes hundreds of pages to analyzing the proper functions of government and how to pay for them. Nor should we be surprised that Adam Smith spent most of his years after finishing *The Wealth of Nations* as a government official, as a collector of customs revenue in Scotland. That was actually consistent with Smith's view of government and commercial society. The government needed funds. The challenge was how to raise them in a way that was most efficient and least oppressive to those who had to pay the taxes.

Smith's views on the functions of the modern state follow from his analysis of the anticipatable negative consequences of the central institution of modern commercial society, namely, the market.

The spread of the market and the resulting intensification of the division of labor that Smith had discussed at the beginning of *The Wealth of Nations* was the source, or at least the precondition, for much of what was best about modern civilized society. That's how wealth was created—wealth that could eventually result in that universal opulence that Smith advocated.

But the market and the division of labor to which it gave birth was also the root of a number of intrinsic dangers. Smith thought that the role of intellectuals like himself was to alert the public and to alert legislators to those dangers with an eye toward obviating them. One of those dangers dealt with the problem of national defense, a perennial problem in the civic republican tradition—but a problem for Adam Smith too, because Smith shows in *The Wealth of Nations* that the need for national defense grew more urgent with the progress of economic development.

The record of history, Smith showed, showed that as a society grew richer it became a more attractive object of attack by its poor neighbors. At the same time, the division of labor, the very process by which a society became richer, created a style of life that left most men less fit to be soldiers. And so in dealing with the problem of national defense, Smith provides a historical analysis of the development of institutions of defense. This, by the way, was Smith's typical mode of analysis. It was a historical analysis of institutions, and he developed a model of historical stages of society, which was a way of trying to come up with some valid and useful generalizations to show the connections between political, economic, and military, and cultural developments.

It's in this respect, as in many others, that Smith's *Wealth of Nations* covers a much wider range of subjects than became characteristic of the discipline of economics in later centuries. Smith does so because he thinks all of these things are related—that you can't think about economic life without thinking about its ramifications for defense and vice versa.

Here is Smith's model of four stages of society and the various kinds of economic and military institutions that each entailed.

The first, most primitive stage was what Smith called the "stage of hunters and fishers." It's the same as what modern anthropologists now call the "stage of hunters and gatherers."

The second stage was that of "nomadic shepherds without commerce." Smith argues that in both of these stages, the stage of hunters and fishers and the stage of nomadic shepherds, every man is a warrior, as well as a hunter. And the skills that they needed for their civilian economic pursuits—that is to say, hunting, fishing, shepherding, riding a horse, and so on—were closely related to the kinds of skills needed for collective military defense. In that sense, there wasn't much of a gap between the economic forces of society and its military needs. Not only was there not central government, but there wasn't need for central government to provide much in the way of special funds for defense.

The third, more advanced stage of society, beyond the stage of nomadic shepherds, was the stage of "settled agriculture," where people worked the land, owned property, but without much commerce or manufacturing. Here, too, Smith argued, the way of life that most people pursued, at least most men pursued, in their day-to-day occupations more or less fitted them for military service. Working in agriculture, working on the land entailed hard physical labor, entailed being out in open-air conditions, and that kind of labor in those kinds of conditions were the kind that fit people to adapt easily to the life of a soldier.

In those sorts of societies, Smith points out, wars were usually fought in the months after seed time and before harvest; that is to say, they were fought between the two seasons that were most demanding of agricultural labor. During that period, most young and able-bodied men, the kind who could serve as soldiers, would serve as soldiers without additional remuneration. So in that stage of society, too, in the stage of settled agriculture, war didn't involve a great deal of additional expense to government.

In medieval Europe under the feudal law, as Smith points out, the sovereign wars were usually conducted by great lords and their retainers at the lords' expense. Once again, the direct cost to the national government was relatively low.

But now there was a new stage of history, that of commercial society characterized by a market economy, increasing urbanization, and an intensive division of labor. At this time in history, war becomes more expensive for government. First of all, that's because of the relationship between people's civil occupations—their occupations in the day-to-day economy—the relationship between those and military service.

Now, in this commercial society, when most men are no longer farmers but increasingly things like smiths, or carpenters, or weavers, it meant that any time spent soldiering was a substantial blow to familial income. If the smith had to go and be a soldier elsewhere, that was time when he wasn't making goods and selling them, so it was a blow to his family's income.

Not only that, but Smith argues that the nature of farming is changed in a commercial economy. It's more labor intensive. Farmers are more likely to devote more of their time to their livelihood. And so it's more expensive for people to leave their civil occupations to go and fight. Not only that, but men were less prepared for war by their ordinary day-to-day occupations. Those occupations left them less time to devote to military exercises because any time taken away from market-related activity was income lost. They couldn't afford to go off to war in large numbers at their own expense. Not only that, but the kinds of occupations that they engaged in, which were increasingly indoor occupations involving, perhaps, less heavy work, certainly not involving day-to-day activities like horseback riding or hunting, these kinds of day-to-day activities left them less and less prepared to be soldiers.

In short, Smith writes, "the great body of the people becomes altogether unwarlike." And this situation, where the great body of the people are no longer fitted by their natural occupation to be soldiers, occurs at the very time when their growing collective wealth is likely to provoke the invasion of more primitive neighboring states. So, Smith thought, as a much later theorist, Leon Trotsky, put it, "You may not be interested in war, but war is interested in you." That is to say, the natural history of social and cultural advance up through commercial society created the potential for national disaster, for the conquest of the civilized and the refined by the rude and the barbarous.

For Smith and for his contemporaries in Scotland, this was no hypothetical situation. It was actually the great historical norm to which past advanced societies in the West had succumbed, like ancient Rome. Indeed, Smith and his contemporaries had experienced it themselves to some degree.

In 1745, the Gaelic clans of the Scottish Highlands were at a much lower level of social and economic advance, and were much more suited by their day-to-day life for war. These Gaelic clans attacked and nearly defeated the more advanced English-speaking commercial areas of the Scottish Lowlands where Smith and his contemporaries lived.

Yet Smith believed that the very advance of the division of labor and opulence made it possible to avoid another disaster, another reversal of civilization comparable to the decline of Rome. He reasoned that like other human activities, the art of war becomes more complex with the division of labor. It requires more specialization. The problem, as Smith saw it, was it couldn't be in the interest of private individuals to devote themselves fully to preparing for war because that brought no profit in peacetime. So he says it's only through the wise policy of the state that the state can attract some individuals to devote themselves fully to military matters by the creation of a permanent army, what in the 18th century was called a "standing army."

He thought that a modern commercial society might be able to avoid some of these disastrous effects suffered by precedents like Rome because it had another advantage in fighting wars. An advanced commercial society was richer, and the development of modern firearms had made the preparation for war ever-more expensive, and that gave an additional advantage to those nations that were wealthier.

Smith's acute historical awareness of the link between national defense and the preservation of civilization led him to insist, in some cases, on the primacy of defense over economic considerations in trade policy. Take his views on the Navigation Acts, for example. You remember that these laws that had been passed in the 17th century made it mandatory to use English ships to import goods from Europe or from the colonies into England. On the whole, Smith was highly critical of the Navigation Acts, but he approved of those provisions because he argued that those provisions gave British ships and sailors a monopoly on the transportation of British goods, and that insured that there would be a supply of sailors and ships necessary for British defense. And so Smith endorses this aspect of the Navigation Acts, despite the fact that they harm the economic interest of British consumers, who were forced to pay a higher price for imported goods as a result.

Smith thought that in a great modern state, a large portion of government revenue would necessarily go to the preparation for war and the protection of commerce, but keep in mind that while Smith was a principal believer in the need for national defense and a standing army, one of the main attractions of free trade for him, as we've seen, is that it would create more peaceful relations between nations, thus making war less likely.

Next to providing for the national defense against other sovereign states, the most important function of government was to provide justice and security under the law. Because it was only security of property, Smith reminded his readers that made it worthwhile for every individual to undertake that effort to better his own condition. Just as the scale of expenditures for military expenditures rose as society became more advanced, so did the costs of administering justice. It was only the state that protected property and hence made "private property" possible. Smith thought that those people with more property actually had a greater interest in maintaining the state, and he reminds his readers of that in *The Wealth of Nations*, that those who were wealthier could enjoy their income only because of the protection provided by the state. It's on these grounds that he argued that the rich ought to be taxed at a higher rate than the poor. Here's the way he puts it:

> Whenever there is great property, there is great inequality. ... The affluence of the rich excites the indignation of the poor, who are often [both] driven by want, and prompted by envy, to invade his possessions. It is only under the shelter of the civil magistrate that the owner of that valuable property, which is acquired by the labour of many years, or perhaps of many successive generations, can sleep a single night in security. He is at all times surrounded by unknown enemies, whom, though he [has] never provoked, he can never appease, and from whose injustice he can be protected only by the powerful arm of the civil magistrate continually held up to chastise it.

You will notice that here Smith takes Rousseau's argument, the argument that government exists to protect the rich against the poor.

But for Smith this isn't an argument against government. He's not saying that there's something intrinsically unjust about having a situation of inequality. He wants to remind the rich, however, that they are secure in their riches, as is everyone else secure in their property, only because of the state.

Another function of government that Smith thought was bound to expand with the advance of commercial society was the provision of what Smith calls "institutions for facilitating the commerce of society." It's what nowadays we call "infrastructure." So facilities like roads, canals, bridges, and harbors—these are facilities that we often take for granted, but they are, in fact, a necessary prerequisite for having advanced commerce.

These are institutions that Smith argued were advantageous for society as a whole, but they couldn't be erected privately because they were too expensive, or too unprofitable for individuals or even groups of investors to provide. So government had to play the main role in providing for infrastructure.

In other words then, *The Wealth of Nations* was much concerned with what in the language of modern economics are called "public goods." By providing for defense, justice, and infrastructure, government created the preconditions for a market economy, and for what Smith calls "that universal opulence which extends itself to the lowest ranks of the people."

The role of government went further yet, because Smith thought that the very process that brought about an increase in national wealth was fraught with negative cultural consequences, which it was up to the legislator to anticipate and up to the intellectual to make the policymakers aware of, so that the negative effects of commercial society could be mitigated and ameliorated.

As you recall, much of the early part of *The Wealth of Nations* is about how the spread of the market makes possible a greater division of labor, thus increasing human productivity. But that same process of the division of labor had negative effects as well, especially upon manual workers. Remember that Adam Smith was writing at a time when there was no general education, when young children could be sent into the factory to work, and when the hours of work in manufacturing left workers with little leisure time.

Smith noted that the intellect, that is, the intellectual life of most men was formed largely by their day-to-day work. And then he makes this shocking observation. As you hear it, keep in mind those people working in the pin factory. Here's what Smith says:

> The man whose whole life is spent in performing a few simple operations ... has no occasion to exert his understanding. ... He naturally loses, therefore, the habit of such exertion, and generally becomes as stupid and ignorant as it is possible for a human creature to become. The torpor of his mind renders him not only incapable of relishing or bearing a part in any rational conversation, but of conceiving any generous, noble, or tender sentiment, and consequently of forming any just judgment concerning many even of the ordinary duties of private life. Of the great and extensive interests of his country he is altogether incapable of judging; and unless very particular pains have been taken to render him otherwise, he is equally incapable of defending his country in war. ... His dexterity at his own particular trade seems, in this manner, to be acquired at the expense of his intellectual, social, and martial virtues. But in every improved and civilized society this is the state into which the laboring poor, that is, the great body of the people, must necessarily fall unless government takes some pains to prevent it.

Now this is a harrowing portrait, really a frightening portrait of the narrowing effects of the division of labor on the human psyche and the human soul. If it were Adam Smith's final judgment on the inevitable cultural consequences of commercial society on the majority of the population, then his verdict about capitalism would certainly have been that its gains were outweighed by the losses, if that was the sort of person that was inevitably going to be produced in large numbers by the system.

Indeed, this quote, ripped from its context, has frequently been cited by opponents of capitalism, including Marx, as testimony to the inevitable alienating effects of capitalism, testimony offered by its most brilliant sympathetic analysts.

The key to Smith's purposes in this gloomily one-sided portrait lies in the last phrase, "unless government takes some pains to prevent it." Smith was, among other things, a professor of rhetoric, and he knew how to write in such a way as to evoke certain emotions in his audience. Smith here is trying to get his readers to act to prevent this scenario. He wants them to lay out money for the purpose, so he has to alarm them in order to motivate them. Because as an antidote to the kind of mental degradation caused by the division of labor, Smith recommended the encouragement of universal public schooling, largely at public expense, so that even those in the lower ranks of society could acquire the essential skills of reading, of writing, and of arithmetic.

Again, here's a suggestion that might seem self-evident to us, but it was deeply at odds with the prevailing wisdom of the dominant classes in Britain at the time. They feared that it would discourage deference, that if people could read and write they wouldn't look up to their natural superiors.

Smith had a more democratic vision. He didn't suggest making schooling compulsory, but he offered a plan to make it more accessible and more useful, and to provide incentives for parents to educate their children. Now you might say, why were such incentives necessary? Why would there have to be incentives for parents to send their children to get schooling? Isn't that what they would naturally have done?

The answer is no. Part of the effect of the rise of the division of labor was that there were forms of manufacturing that required repetitive work—work that adults, and especially adult men, often revolted against doing—and often, therefore, women and children were hired to do that sort of work. And those children could actually earn money, so families had an economic incentive to send children not to school, but into the factory, and therefore Smith wants to create economic incentives for families to send their children to school.

The division of labor, therefore, not only stunted the intellectual abilities of workers by narrowing their horizons, it created economic incentives for the neglect of any formal education by providing work the children could do in factories instead of going to school. And so Smith talks about the need for the public to, as he puts it, to "facilitate … encourage, and … even impose upon almost the whole body of the people the necessity of acquiring those most essential parts of education," that is to say, reading, writing, and arithmetic.

In formulating recommendations for public policy, Smith once again examined the historical record and the comparative record to suggest institutional means to counteract the anticipatable negative consequences of new developments, in this case, the anticipatable negative consequences of the division of labor on the laboring masses.

Smith's first educational recommendation called for the creation of public schools that would be maintained partly at public expense and partly by very low fees. In addition to the benefits of education for the individual, Smith thought, it was also a prime political consideration for the state to have a more educated populace. Smith believed that the more educated the population, the less they would be prone to religious zealotry and to religious civil war.

He also thought that a more educated population, capable of reading, would be in a better position to make political judgments as citizens. He hoped that they would be able to more critically examine those self-interested claims made by one or another economic group or political faction.

So Adam Smith does maintain many elements of the civic republican tradition in a form more amenable to a commercial society. He emphasizes, for example, the importance of collective defense—not as a highest value, but as a necessary evil that policymakers have to think about.

He deals with trying to encourage citizens to be able to participate in government, in this case, by trying to bring about that spread of education so that more people would be in a position to participate in the political process. And indeed, the whole structure of *The Wealth of Nations* is intended to motivate policymakers toward the general interest despite all those pressures on them to favor one or another economic group. That task, Smith thought, would be a difficult one, but he obviously thought that it was possible; otherwise, he wouldn't have written *The Wealth of Nations*.

So Adam Smith didn't think that every result of the market was good, nor did he think that every action of government was bad. He thought, as we've seen, that the spread of the market could make men better off, could bring about that universal opulence. But that depended on the governmental provision of some public goods, as we've seen. He also thought that the spread of the market created problems of its own. It was the proper role of intellectuals, he thought, to try to analyze those problems, and to try to suggest how they might be alleviated.

Smith thought that the spread of the market, the spread of commercial society could make men not only better off, but actually could make men better. We'll turn to those issues in our next lecture.

Lecture Ten
Smith on Moral and Immoral Capitalism

Scope:

Smith thought that commercial society had the potential of making people not only better off materially, but also of improving their character. It had a propensity to promote certain positive character traits, such as industriousness and probity. It held out the possibility of a society in which most people would be more self-controlled, prudent, and free. That was no small achievement. Under the right institutional conditions, a capitalist society could make people better, as well as better off. But where the rule of law was lacking—or where there was inequality before the law, as in the case of slavery or of colonial companies—commerce could lead to immoral outcomes.

Outline

I. Adam Smith was a moral philosopher particularly interested in the question of how men become moral (i.e., the social processes through which they develop desirable character traits, or virtues).
   A. He did not think that "virtue" is a single character trait but rather that there are a variety of desirable character traits, some of which the market tends to cultivate and some of which it does not.
   B. One important element in Smith's evaluation of commercial society and its relationship to the virtues was that he didn't think that poverty was ennobling.

II. Smith thought that a well-functioning market, by leading to greater prosperity, would make it more likely that people would act with benevolence.
   A. He believed that moving beyond a society of scarcity would allow people the mental space to sympathize with others, to try to put themselves in the shoes of others and act more benevolently toward them.
   B. In this sense, Smith takes the Christian virtue of charity and translates it into the more worldly form of benevolence toward others.

III. Smith thought that the market activity itself tends to produce certain desirable character traits.
   A. Business leads the merchant to develop habits of "order, economy, and attention … [that] render him much fitter to execute, with profit and success, any project of improvement."
   B. The development of regular and frequent market relations, Smith thought, tends to lead to honesty, or what he called "probity."
   C. Recurrent market relations guide self-interest toward the keeping of promises. This makes honesty the best policy.
   D. The seller wants to cultivate trust, and the best way to do that is to act in a way that is trustworthy. So, too, with punctuality.
   E. Because character traits are created by habit, there is a spillover effect from economic relations, and the habits of honesty and punctuality are carried over into other areas of life.

IV. Smith thought that the master virtue was "self-command," or what we would call "self-control."
   A. The market tends to lead toward self-control through the pursuit of self-interest in the market.
   B. The quality of character that the market promotes is prudence: the disciplined pursuit of self-interest and the ability to defer short-term gratification for long-term benefit.
   C. To the degree that in a commercial society every person becomes a merchant, the qualities of self-control, commitment to honoring promises, and punctuality are spread through society.

V. As an enlightened thinker, Smith valued freedom of the individual and autonomy (i.e., the ability to exercise control over one's fate).
   A. He thought there was a link between individual autonomy and self-support through legally free labor.
   B. Thomas Carlyle—and later Marx and Engels—would decry the system of mutual appeals to self-interest as the "cash nexus."

- C. But there are two positive sides of the cash nexus: the freedom and self-determination that come from having cash, and the fact that relations based on cash do not involve the total subordination of one individual to the will of another (the characteristic forms of human relations under slavery or serfdom).
- D. It was the combination of legal security of person and property, free labor, and the market that produced the virtues that Smith valued in commercial society as it had developed in northwestern Europe.

VI. These priorities are evident in Smith's discussion of slavery and serfdom.
- A. Commercial development by itself did not produce liberty or free labor.
- B. Slavery and serfdom, Smith reasoned, appeal to some of the most pernicious human passions.
- C. For Smith, the most liberating effect of the rise of commercial society was its replacement of direct and open-ended personal dependency with the cash nexus, the contractual relations that limit the entitlement of people to dominate one another.
- D. Smith's moral preference for commercial society based upon free wage labor was that it made it necessary for everyone to bargain with everyone, to persuade them to work, rather than being able to command them to work in the way characteristic of slavery or serfdom.

VII. Another example of what Smith regarded as a pernicious form of commerce was the East India Company.
- A. The growth of European trade with China, India, Japan, and the East Indies, Smith reasoned, should have been of great benefit to the consumers of Europe.
- B. But it had been of only limited advantage, because it was conducted exclusively by monopolies, such as the East India Companies of Holland, England, and France.
- C. If these monopolies had kept Europe from gaining the full potential benefits of transcontinental trade, the consequences for some of its colonies were even more negative, Smith showed.

VIII. Smith's evaluation of the moral effects of capitalism, or what he called "commercial society," was mixed.
  - **A.** Commercial society, in Smith's portrait, did not make most people highly virtuous and noble—but then, he thought no society could.
  - **B.** While Smith thought that commercial society tended to produce certain commendable character traits (virtues) such as prudence and self-control and a certain level of concern for others, he did not think that a society that produced only those character traits would thrive.
  - **C.** Society needed at least some people with greater virtues, like bravery and fortitude, without which it could not defend itself.
  - **D.** One purpose of Smith's *Theory of Moral Sentiments* was to encourage these greater virtues that were not provided by the market itself.
  - **E.** Perhaps the main purpose of *The Wealth of Nations* was to produce more informed legislators and statesmen, who could better foresee the results of their actions.
  - **F.** Here too we see elements of the civic republican tradition, now reformulated to be more compatible with a market-based society.

Suggested Reading:

Smith, *The Wealth of Nations*, Book 4, chap. 7; Book 5, chap. 1.

Muller, *Adam Smith in His Time and Ours*, chap. 10.

Muthu, "Adam Smith's Critique of International Trading Companies."

Questions to Consider:

1. What sorts of desirable character traits are fostered by the market itself?
2. What sorts of socially desirable character traits are not fostered by the market?

Lecture Ten—Transcript
Smith on Moral and Immoral Capitalism

Adam Smith was a moral philosopher, and as such, he was interested in the question of what it meant to be moral. He was particularly interested in the question of how men become moral; that is, what are the social processes through which they develop desirable character traits, or as they're also known, virtues?

Smith didn't think that virtue was a single, unitary trait, that there was one character trait to which all other virtues were connected. Rather, he thought that there were a variety of desirable character traits, and some of these character traits he thought the market tended to foster and to cultivate, and some of them it does not. Let's look at Adam Smith's moral evaluation of commercial society.

One important element in Smith's evaluation of commercial society and its relationship to the virtues was that he didn't think that poverty was ennobling. As he puts it, "Before we can feel much for others, we must in some measure be at ease ourselves. If our own misery pinches us very severely, we have no leisure to attend to that of our neighbour." And so Smith thought that a well-functioning market, by leading to greater prosperity, would make it more likely that people would act with benevolence—a secularized version, in some ways, of the Christian virtue of charity.

Smith thought that moving beyond a society of poverty and scarcity would allow people the mental space to think more about others, to sympathize with others, to try to put themselves in the shoes of others, and therefore to act more benevolently toward them. In that sense, Smith takes this Christian virtue of charity and translates it into the more worldly form of benevolence toward others.

Some people find this line of analysis hard to believe. Is it true that a society that is richer, or that individuals who are better off, are likely to be more benevolent toward others? Think of how often philanthropic movements were led by those who had attained a good deal of material comfort, leaving them the mental space to think about others, sometimes people who are quite distant from them. Think, for example, of the antislavery crusades of the 19th century. Indeed, think of how often contemporary philanthropic efforts are spearheaded by people who are materially comfortable, or perhaps actually well-to-do.

Smith thought that the market itself, that market activity itself, tends to produce certain desirable character traits. In commercial society, based upon exchange, every man, Smith writes, "becomes in some measure a merchant." To get a sense of Smith's evaluation of the moral effects of commercial society, it's useful to look at his description of the kind of character traits that merchants are most likely to develop.

In *The Wealth of Nations*, the portrait of merchants tends to be quite critical as people who are out for their own self-interest at the expense of the general interest. But elsewhere in his work, especially in *The Theory of Moral Sentiments* and in some of the works that were unpublished in his day, Smith reflects more broadly on the kinds of character traits that business activity is likely to develop. In the first instance, in merchants, but then more broadly in a commercial society where everybody becomes a merchant to some degree because they're selling something. They may be selling a product; they may be selling their services; they may be selling their labor; but everybody insofar as they're involved in the market as sellers becomes to some degree or another a merchant.

Smith says that business leads the merchant to develop certain habits, certain character traits, those that he calls "order, economy, and attention … [that] render him much fitter to execute, with profit and success, any project of improvement." Let's unpack that a bit.

Business tends to develop the character trait of order; that is to say, to succeed in business you have to learn to become organized. "Economy," that's used in the sense of learning to try to maximize efficiency by matching means and ends, or getting the most output with the least input. "Attention" means learning to devote oneself to the task at hand. These are the kinds of character traits that Smith thinks merchant activity develops, and once one has learned these character traits in one's occupation, they tend to spill over into other activities. So these are the kinds of character traits that tend to characterize merchants, and tend to characterize everybody insofar as they become merchants because they have something to sell in a commercial society.

Smith thought that the development of regular and frequent market relations tends to lead to honesty, or what in the language of the 18th century he calls "probity." That is to say, self-interest guides us toward the keeping of promises. In a situation of recurrent market relations, self-interest makes honesty the best policy. And here the emphasis is on recurrent market relations. If market relations are rare, or if they're a one-shot deal, then the incentives of self-interest are different.

Take the case of the street merchant on the street in Times Square trying to sell a watch that he claims to be a Rolex to an unsuspecting tourist from out of town. The merchant in that case, the seller, has little incentive to be honest. His self-interest leads him to try to get the maximum amount of profit. He hopes indeed that he's not going to have an ongoing relationship with that customer. This is supposed to a one-shot deal. Under those circumstances there is no incentive for that seller to be honest. He wants to make a killing. He wants to get the highest profit that he can on that one deal, under the assumption that he'll never see the buyer again.

But if the seller is looking for regular, or ongoing, sales, then the structure of incentives is very different. Then, in pursuit of his own self-interest, he has every incentive to satisfy the customer. He has every incentive to satisfy the customer in regard to price, in regard to the reliability of the product that's being sold—don't sell it as a Rolex if it's not. He has every incentive to have a satisfied customer in terms of the quality of the sales experience itself, because in those situations of recurrent market activity the seller is less interested in the profit from any one sale than in having the customer return time and again.

In short, in situations of recurrent market activity, what the seller wants to cultivate is trust in his customers and in his potential customers, and the best way to cultivate trust is to act in a way that is trustworthy. So the merchant, then, has an incentive, Smith says, to act with probity, with honesty. So, too, the merchant has an incentive, as does everyone when they're involved in market relations where they're trying to sell something, including their labor and services—the seller has an incentive to act with punctuality, which Smith says is another character virtue that gets developed in a market society. You want to act with punctuality because you don't want to alienate the buyer by being late.

Here, too, just as in the situation of the pin factory, there were negative spillover effects in the sense that the kinds of mental traits that were created under the division of labor in the factory had a deadening effect. Here, too, Smith thinks that there are spillover effects from economic relations to other relations. In this case, they're largely positive spillover effects. Character traits are a result of habit, and once you get into the habit in your day-to-day business relations of acting with honesty, with punctuality, with efficiency, and so on, Smith thinks you're likely to carry these traits over into other areas of life, and in that sense these sorts of virtues spill over into the rest of commercial society.

Smith thought that the master virtue, so to speak, the virtue that makes all the others really effective, is what he called "self-command," or what we would call "self-control." He thought it was fine to be benevolent, charitable, sympathetic, and so on, but without self-control, those virtues aren't worth very much. You can't really execute them. And one of Smith's key findings is that the market itself is a sort of disciplining institution of society. The market tends to lead toward self-control through the pursuit of self-interest in the market. That's because in order to become successful in his economic exchanges with others, the individual is led to develop a certain level of self-control, not an exalted level of self-mastery, not the most noble level of self-mastery, but a certain level of self-control that Smith calls "propriety." By that he means essentially acting in a way that takes into account not only your point of view and your emotions, but the point of view of those with whom you have economic relations.

Remember that the division of labor leads to a mutual dependence in society. We're constantly acting to some degree or another as merchants. We depend to some degree or another on others for the things we want to sell and the things we want to buy, and Smith says that this leads people to adapt their behavior to the expectations of others, and often enough to control themselves, to exercise self-control over themselves, in order to bring their behavior down to a level that is pleasing to the person that they're dealing with.

To produce a satisfied customer you have to learn to see things from the perspective of the customer. You have to adapt your behavior to take into account the customer's point of view. You might be angry, annoyed, impatient—but if you want to keep your customer, or if you're working for someone, if you want to keep your job, or if someone is working for you and you want to retain an employee—under all those cases you have to learn to restrain your anger, your annoyance, your impatience. You have to engage in self-control.

Similarly, in order to keep a job, one has to engage in continuous work, and that requires a certain amount of self-control as well. So Smith thought that the qualities of character that the market tends to promote are, above all, prudence, or prudential forms of behavior, that is, the disciplined pursuit of self-interest and the ability to defer short-term gratification for longer-term benefits. And to the degree that in a commercial society every man becomes a merchant, these qualities of self-control, commitment to honoring promises, punctuality, and so on are spread through society.

As an enlightened thinker, Smith valued freedom of the individual, autonomy, the ability to exercise some control over one's own fate, and he thought that there was a link between individual autonomy and supporting oneself through legally free labor. Let's look again at the famous statement near the beginning of *The Wealth of Nations*, but now with the addition of the next sentence.

> It is not from the benevolence of the butcher, the brewer, or the baker, that we expect our dinner, but from their regard to their own interest. We address ourselves, not to their humanity but to their self-love, and never talk to them of our own necessities but of their advantages.

And now here's the new part: "Nobody but a beggar chooses to depend chiefly upon the benevolence of his fellow-citizens." Now, this passage is, of course, most famous as a statement of the potential utility of self-interest, but notice the assertion at the end. Dependence on the benevolence of others is morally degrading and, hence, something we should try to avoid, if possible.

The 19th-century author Thomas Carlyle, and later Marx and Engels, would decry this system of mutual appeals to self-interest as the "cash nexus." But one positive side of the cash nexus is the freedom and self-determination that comes from having cash. The second positive side of the cash nexus is the fact that relations based on the exchange of cash don't involve the total subordination of one individual to the will of another, and that was the characteristic form of human relations under the alternatives, under slavery or serfdom.

Serfdom and slavery were systems of power that left the serf or the slave at the mercy of his owner. Unlike the free laborer, serfs and slaves weren't able to change bosses, and the boss controls one's fate under slavery or under serfdom, not just during work hours, but all of the time. The alternative, then, to serfdom and to slavery was a government that was strong enough to guarantee equality before the law.

Smith thought that the monopoly of physical power by the government was a prerequisite of liberty and also of prosperity. Otherwise, we're either unprotected in our person or property, or as in the case of serfdom, we owe our protection to our owner or master, which robs us of a sense of personal autonomy.

So for Smith it was this combination of legal security of person and property, of free labor and the market, that together produced the virtues that he valued in commercial society as it was developing in northwestern Europe. Those priorities are quite evident when we look at Smith's discussions of slavery and serfdom because what we see from that is that commercial development by itself or under the wrong conditions didn't produce liberty or free labor. That was shown by the case of eastern Europe, where serfdom was still widespread. The master class of serf owners on their land produced goods for the international capitalist market, especially grain. In eastern Europe, the absence of strong central government had allowed commercial development to reinforce what Smith called the "urge to domineer," resulting in commercial development; that is, the grain was sold into the international market using unfree labor.

Slavery and serfdom, Smith reasoned, appeal to some of the most pernicious human passions. He says, "The pride of man makes him love to domineer. ... Wherever the law allows it, and the nature of the work can afford it ... he will generally prefer the services of slaves to that of freemen." Smith's abhorrence of relations of direct personal dependence made him loath slavery. There are parts of *The Wealth of Nations* that were reprinted time and again by abolitionists in the 19th century.

Smith describes the slave trader and slave owners as "the refuse of the [jails] ... of Europe ... wretches who possess the virtues neither of the countries which they come from, nor of those which they go to, and whose levity, brutality, and baseness, so justly expose them to the contempt of the vanquished."

So for Smith the most liberating moral effect of the rise of commercial society was its replacement of direct and open-ended personal dependency with the cash nexus, that is to say, the contractual relation that limits the entitlement of men to dominate one another. So individual autonomy was an important value for Smith, and he thought that that autonomy was endangered by this negative human passion to dominate and control others. Smith thought that some people, at least, get a certain pleasure from what he calls "the love of domination and authority over others," or as he puts it, "a certain desire of having others below one, and the pleasure it gives one to have some persons whom he can order to do his work rather than be obliged to persuade others to bargain with him."

That last phrase is particularly important. Smith's moral preference for commercial society, based on free wage labor, was that it made it necessary for everyone to bargain with everyone else. It made it necessary for everyone to persuade others to do what they wanted them to do, to persuade them to work rather than being able to command them to work in the way that the noble lord could, or in the way that the slave owner could.

Another example of what Smith regarded as pernicious forms of commerce in his day, like the kinds of commerce carried on by serf owners, and even more so the kinds of commerce carried on by slave owners, was the East India Company.

The East India Company, you'll remember, was one of those companies that had been granted a monopoly on trade with an entire region of the world. In Smith's day, the British East India Company was the largest commercial enterprise in the world, and it comes in for a great deal of criticism in *The Wealth of Nations*, as do the other chartered monopoly companies.

Remember that Smith's sentiments were cosmopolitan. He was interested in the well-being of his fellow Scots, of his fellow Britons, but he was also interested in the well-being of those in other parts of the world, and he argued that the growth of European trade with China, with India, with Japan, with the East Indies should have been of great benefit to the consumers of Europe. But he argued that while it had brought some benefit, those relations had only been of limited advantage, and they had been of limited advantage because they were conducted exclusively by monopolies, like the East India Company of England, or of Holland, or of France.

To carry on their trade monopoly, these companies established military control over foreign regions and came to govern foreign regions. The result, Smith thought, was detrimental to the home country and ruinous to those subject non-European nations. He argued that the consumers of the home country, so of France and Holland and Britain, suffered all the disadvantages that came from having an exclusive supplier that was unrestrained by the forces of market competition. Since these companies controlled the supply of the goods that they imported, say from India into Britain, they made sure that supply would remain lower than demand. That would keep prices high, and that was good for their profits but bad for British consumers. So Smith thought that these monopoly companies had kept Europe from gaining the full potential benefits of transcontinental trade. He thought that the consequences for some of the colonies were even more negative.

In an attempt to restrict the supply of Indian goods that were exported to Europe, the East India Company had deliberately destroyed parts of India's production and had destroyed excess production in an attempt to keep supply low. And if demand remained the same and supply was low, then price would go up. So it benefited the company but no one else.

Smith argued that these companies that were now acting as de facto rulers of entire areas of the world were morally abhorrent and a counterproductive force. He argued that a true sovereign understood that his own revenue depended upon the wealth of the nation that he governed and that he would try to promote that wealth through freer trade, but he says that a company of merchants that has become the rulers of a territory, like India, seemed incapable of grasping such considerations.

They used their political power only to buy more cheaply in India in order to increase company profits. So the effect of company rule, Smith concluded, of companies like the East India Company was to stunt the growth of the Indian economy. So for Smith there are forms of commerce that he thought were pernicious, morally abhorrent, including, as we've seen, the activity of the largest corporation of his day.

Adam Smith's evaluation of the moral effects of capitalism, or what he called "commercial society," was mixed. For the first time in history, commercial society created the possibility that most men could live a morally decent existence. In their quest to improve their well-being through market activity, they were learning valuable virtues: to defer gratification, to control their appetites, and developing what Smith called a "steady perseverance in the practice of frugality, industry, and application, though directed to no other purpose than the acquisition of fortune."

So commercial society, in Smith's portrait, does not make most men highly virtuous and noble, but then he thought no society could. It did hold out the possibility of a society in which most people would be more self-controlled, more prudent, and more free. That was no small achievement. Under the right institutional conditions, a capitalist society, he thought, could make men better as well as making them better off. But where the rule of law was lacking, or where there was inequality before the law, as in the case of slavery or of colonial companies, commerce could lead to immoral outcomes.

While Smith thought that commercial society tended to produce certain commendable character traits, certain commendable virtues like prudence and self-control, and a certain level of concern for others, he didn't think that a society that produced only those character traits would thrive. In other words, the character traits produced by the market, while often desirable, were not enough to create a really good and flourishing society. Society, he thought, needed at least some people with greater virtues, virtues like bravery and fortitude, without which it couldn't defend itself. It needed at least some citizens and legislators who were devoted to the public wheel, to the public interest—citizens and legislators who were both prudent and well-informed.

Part of the purpose of *The Theory of Moral Sentiments* was to encourage these greater virtues that were not provided by the market itself. And perhaps the main purpose of *The Wealth of Nations* was to produce more informed legislators and statesmen who could better foresee the results of their actions. Here again we see elements of the civic republican tradition now reformulated to be more compatible with a market-based society.

In some respects, Adam Smith's project was a success. *The Wealth of Nations* was one of the most influential works of its time, indeed, one of the most influential works of all time. It was soon incorporated into the curriculum of Thomas Jefferson's new University of Virginia in the new United States. It was translated within a decade or two into most European languages, including

German. And in German-speaking Europe, it was incorporated into the curriculum of the University of Königsberg and other institutions at which future leaders of Prussia and of other German states were trained. But its conclusions and its recommendations remained a matter of contention, as we'll see when we discuss Justus Möser in Germany and Alexander Hamilton in the United States.

But first, let's look at Smith's contemporary, Edmund Burke, who agreed with most of Smith's economic analysis but suggested that in the wrong combination, the spread of capitalism might destroy the institutional foundations on which commercial society rested.

Lecture Eleven
Conservatism and Advanced Capitalism—Burke

Scope:

Edmund Burke (1729–1797) offered a conservative analysis of the hazards posed by some forms of capitalism to the politics and culture of an already commercialized society. As a member of Parliament, he became a leading critic of the British East India Company. He argued that the company's agents, in search of gain and unrestrained by the inherited culture of England, were riding roughshod over traditional Indian society. Burke then applied this analysis to the French Revolution in *Reflections on the Revolution in France* (1790), his seminal work of conservative thought. He argued that the revolution was propelled into dangerous radicalism by a combination of radical intellectuals and newly rich entrepreneurs who were oriented toward risk and failed to appreciate the existing institutions of their society.

Outline

I. Edmund Burke's *Reflections on the Revolution in France* (1790) is the single most influential work of conservative thought published from his day to ours.

   A. Along with Burke's arguments for the continuity of established institutions as conducive to human happiness, *Reflections* is best known for its critique of the pernicious role of intellectuals in political life.

   B. Less well known is the book's sustained contention that "men of money" were undermining the institutions of the state and the church.

   C. Burke was among the most important intellectuals in European politics, and he championed capitalist economic development from his earliest published writings until his last days.

   D. Unraveling why Burke wrote one of the most biting critiques of both intellectuals and entrepreneurs will lead us into the ever-changing forms of tension between capitalism and conservatism.

II. The society Burke sought to conserve was a hierarchical society that was already highly commercialized.
  A. Burke shared the preference of Voltaire and Smith for commercial society over its historical alternatives.
  B. He concluded, however, that Smith had overlooked the institutional and cultural prerequisites of a commercial society, and that radicalized intellectuals presented a threat to the foundations upon which modern commercial society rested.
  C. The problem was with intellectuals who had an unreasonable conception of reason, and of men of money whose self-interest was unrestrained by legal or cultural codes.
  D. Understanding how Edmund Burke arrived at that position requires a quick journey through his career, from his birth in Dublin (1729), when Ireland lacked a politically connected native elite that was devoted to economic growth, to his entry into politics as a member of Parliament (1765–1794).

III. As the intellectual engine of the Rockingham Whigs, Burke's function was to enunciate principles, to influence Parliament through his speeches and reports, and to influence extra-Parliamentary opinion.
  A. Burke's greatest influence was exerted via the new means of cultural production through which "public opinion" was created.
  B. Burke was very conscious that what counted as public opinion was heavily influenced by intellectuals.
  C. From the beginning of his public career to its end, Burke warned of the potentially disastrous social and political results of intellect gone astray.
  D. As a conservative, Burke argued that radical change was dangerous because institutions and customs often interlinked, so intentionally changing one might bring about negative unintended consequences.
  E. The attempt to subject all institutions to rational scrutiny could have its own negative consequences, by destroying the legitimacy of existing institutions without being able to provide workable new ones.

IV. Burke was in substantial agreement with Adam Smith about self-interest, but Burke was a defender of aristocracy as providing a kind of anchor, slowing down the pace of change in a commercializing society.
   A. Burke argued that those engaged in commerce, who stem from more modest backgrounds, have more to gain from change and are more likely to do so without the proper caution.
   B. Burke had a dynamic view of commercial society, believing that as new interests arose, they ought to be represented in the political system.
   C. He was suspicious of too great a role for new-moneyed men, who lacked a sufficient sense of tradition.
   D. He also became a defender of the established Church of England as a repository of inherited culture.

V. As a member of Parliament, Burke became a leading critic of the British East India Company.
   A. He argued that the company's agents in India were unrestrained by the inherited culture of England and were riding roughshod over traditional Indian society.
   B. These men then used their ill-gotten wealth to buy influence in Parliament and prevent governmental scrutiny of their actions.
   C. Burke concluded that commerce unchecked by traditional moral codes could erode the foundations of the political order.

VI. Burke then applied this analysis to the French Revolution in *Reflections*.
   A. Late in 1789, the revolutionary parliament voted to nationalize the assets of the church, and to sell them to pay the national debt.
   B. Writing in an early stage of the revolution, Burke predicted that it would become more radical and more murderous.

- **C.** In Burke's analysis, this is due to the coming together of two forces: politicized intellectuals who wanted to remake society according to their abstract theories and radicalized intellectuals who wanted to undermine the position of the established Catholic Church and its monopoly on education.
- **D.** They were supported by men of money, who now held the national debt and wanted to be sure that it was paid.
- **E.** Burke reasoned that men who made their money through commerce and finance had a mentality that made them too open to the entreaties of radical intellectuals.

VII. Burke argued that the intellectuals' attack on the church would lead to an erosion of cultural constraints.
- **A.** Because inherited cultural codes had come about and been transmitted by the church and the aristocracy, weakening the power of these institutions would create people with more freedom but less self-restraint.
- **B.** This, he predicted, would lead to political radicalization and to barbaric behavior.
- **C.** Burke's main contribution to the debate over capitalism was his notion that commercial society may depend upon inherited institutions that restrain people and make them decent.

VIII. Burke also argued against taking contractual relations as the model of all relations.
- **A.** Contractual relations are the typical relations in the market, and Burke thought a spillover effect on nonmarket relations would be counterproductive.
- **B.** Burke pointed to the importance in some areas of life of noncontractual obligations that applied to the state.
- **C.** He said that not every relationship is like a market-oriented contract that one enters into through choice and that one can get out of when one thinks it's no longer in one's interest: There are political and social institutions.

Suggested Reading:

Burke, *Reflections on the Revolution in France.*

Muller, *Conservatism,* Introduction, Afterword, and selections from Burke.

———, *The Mind and the Market,* chap. 5.

O'Brien, *The Great Melody,* 255–384.

Questions to Consider:

1. Compare the critiques of Adam Smith and Edmund Burke of the East India Company and of moral and immoral forms of capitalism.

2. In the United States, the distinction is often made between those who consider themselves "cultural conservatives" and those who consider themselves "economic conservatives" and tend toward minimal government and unrestrained markets. What ongoing sources of tension between these two varieties of conservatism can be traced back to Burke's thought?

Lecture Eleven—Transcript
Conservatism and Advanced Capitalism—Burke

Edmund Burke's book of 1790, *Reflections on the Revolution in France*, is the single most influential work of conservative thought published from his day to ours. It wasn't the first work of conservative thought, but it has remained the most influential because it struck every chord of conservative sentiment, it rung every chime of conservative analysis, and it enunciated virtually every subsequent theme of conservative ideology.

Along with Burke's arguments for the continuity of established institutions as conducive to human happiness, which is of course the key theme of his *Reflections*, the *Reflections* is best known for its critique of the pernicious role of intellectuals in French political life. Less well known is the book's sustained contention that "men of money," as Burke called them, were undermining the institutions of the state and of the church in France.

Yet Burke, who emerged as the scourge of politicized men of letters and of men of money, was among the most important intellectuals in European politics before 1789, that is, before the French Revolution. And this man who chastised men of money had championed capitalist economic development from his earliest published writings, and continued to do so through his last days. In fact, he advocated a reliance on the profit motive and on the market as the coordinating mechanism of economic life, as did Adam Smith. Why, then, did the foremost intellectual in politics, and one of the foremost advocates of the market, pen one of the most biting critiques of both intellectuals and entrepreneurs?

Unraveling that paradox, or that seeming paradox, will lead us into the tensions between capitalism and conservatism. The tensions between capitalism and conservatism take different forms in different times and places because capitalism changes across time, and so does conservatism. Conservatism varies from one time to another and from one society to another, depending on the institutions that conservatives are trying to conserve, and those institutions have been different in different societies at the same time and in the same society across historical time. We'll see that in this lecture and in the next one.

The society that Edmund Burke sought to conserve was a hierarchical society that was already highly commercialized. It was a society dominated by a landed aristocracy, but a landed aristocracy that was itself very commercially minded. In the next lecture, we'll look at another conservative thinker, Justus Möser, who was trying to conserve a society that was largely precommercial.

If Rousseau was an internal critic of the Enlightenment from the left, so to speak, we can say that Burke and Möser were internal critics of the Enlightenment from the right. I know this will shock some people, but it's true. In many respects Burke, like Möser, was an Enlightenment thinker; that is to say, he shared the premises of Voltaire and Hume and Smith about the desirability of the pursuit of worldly happiness. It's just that Burke, like Möser, differed on the question of how to get there.

But Burke shared a great deal more than that with Voltaire and Hume and Smith. He shared the preference of Voltaire and Smith for a commercial society compared to its historical alternatives. The difference was that he concluded that Smith had overlooked some of the institutional and cultural prerequisites of a commercial society. Burke concluded that radicalized intellectuals presented a threat to the foundations upon which commercial society itself rested. The problem, as Burke conceived of it, was not with intellectuals as such, and not with the market as such. Nor was Burke opposed to the use of reason. His problem was with intellectuals who he thought had an unreasonable conception of reason—that is to say, who overestimated the amount that could be known about society and, hence, underestimated the costs of radical change. And his critique was not of capitalism as such, but of men of money whose self-interest was unrestrained by legal or cultural codes.

Understanding how Edmund Burke arrived at that position, a position that's enunciated in his *Reflections on the Revolution in France*, requires a quick journey through his career.

Burke was born in Dublin in 1729, which made him six years younger than Adam Smith. But Burke's Ireland was very different from Smith's Scotland. Scotland was in the midst of an economic efflorescence led by a class of improving native landowners who were linked to London by a customs union and by close political ties. They were bringing their society along into a more commercial, more opulent society.

Burke's Irish homeland, by contrast, suffered under less propitious political and economic circumstances, because Burke's Ireland lacked a politically connected native elite that was devoted to economic growth. That's because in the 17th century, the British had conquered Ireland and imposed a class of British landowners who had little identification with the larger Irish population, and indeed, who were often absentee landlords.

In one of his earliest published articles, Burke lamented Ireland's economic backwardness, which he attributed to its domination by those landowners who, instead of setting an example of economic improvement, were bent on impoverishing a land whose people they despised.

Young Edmund Burke moved to London and burst onto the intellectual, and then onto the political, stage in several leaps, beginning with the publication in 1756 of his book, *A Vindication of Natural Society*. The book, which was written under a pseudonym and in an ironic tone, was written as if it were by a radical Enlightenment intellectual along the lines of Rousseau. But it was, in fact, a critique of Rousseau and other radical Enlightenment thinkers who sought to do away with existing institutions and who sought to build society anew on an entirely rational basis. As we'll see, that critique, not of rationalism but of the pretensions of rationalism, was an ongoing theme in Burke's work.

The next year, Burke published a book called *A Philosophical Inquiry into the Origin of Our Ideas of the Sublime and Beautiful*, a book that was regarded at the time, and since, as one of the most important 18th-century works on aesthetics.

Not long thereafter, in 1758, Burke launched the *Annual Register*. This was a summary of the major political, literary, social, and artistic events of the preceding year all across Europe. He was something of an intellectual whirlwind. He wrote much of the volume himself through 1763, and he turned the project into a commercial success. In other words, he managed to make a living as a writer in the capitalist market.

By his mid-30s, Burke had achieved the recognition of his fellow men of letters. He was a member of what was known as The Club, a club that included such intellectual luminaries as the writer Samuel Johnson; the painter Joshua Reynolds; and, when he was in London,

Adam Smith himself. But the intellectual and cultural stage was not enough to hold Edmund Burke. He made his way into politics through the only gate open to a man of large talent but modest means, and that was patronage. During much of his long career in Parliament, from 1765 to 1794, Burke owed his seat to aristocratic patronage, in the first instance to Lord Rockingham, who was the head of a political faction known as the Rockingham Whigs.

Like some subsequent conservative politicians, Lord Rockingham had a problem with what a later politician called "the vision thing," and Burke's task was to provide the vision thing. It was as an intellectual that Burke exerted his political influence, and it was as the intellectual engine of the Rockingham faction that he exerted that influence. His function in Parliament was to enunciate principles for the Rockingham faction and then to try to influence Parliament through his speeches and through published reports—and those published reports in turn were read by a larger audience beyond the walls of Parliament.

So Burke's greatest influence was exerted via these new means of cultural production through which public opinion was created, and that, again, was the commerce in books and pamphlets and newspapers that appealed to this newly educated public concerned with Parliamentary and political affairs. Burke was very conscious of the fact that the spread of these commercially distributed means of information had made public opinion into an ever-more important factor in politics, and he was very much aware that what counted as public opinion was heavily influenced by intellectuals.

It was as a combatant in the war of opinion that Burke made his initial appearance on the London intellectual scene when in 1756 he published the book *A Vindication of Natural Society*. From the beginning of his public career to its end, Burke warned of the potentially disastrous social and political results of intellect gone astray, of intellect unaware of its own limits, or intellect that overrated its own powers.

In this first book, he focused on the snares of what he saw as a kind of abstract rationalism, a frame of mind that demanded a rational justification of every existing institution, that rejected out of hand every institution that didn't meet the standards set by theories of justice, and the demand that human society be reconstructed to conform to these abstract theories of justice.

As a conservative—and indeed this is what made him a conservative intellectual—Burke was very sensitive to the pitfalls of radical change. It wasn't against change as such—indeed, he thought reform was part of conserving a society—but he was very sensitive to the pitfalls of radical change. And his argument, which was picked up by so many subsequent conservatives, was that institutions and the customs and habits that go with them are often interlinked, so that by intentionally changing one institution or one custom, one might bring about negative unintended consequences. That is to say, because the links between institutions were often hidden, were often not apparent to the observer by transforming one institution, it could have knock-on effects on other institutions that one didn't want to bring about. In that sense it was an example of unanticipated and unintended negative consequences.

Burke thought that customs and institutions usually existed for good reasons. This is a mode of thought that could be called "historical utilitarianism." It's not his term, but I think it captures what he was about. That is to say, the notion that institutions that have developed through history have developed the way they have, and have come down to us for a reason—that they have some utility, that they have some function. And those institutions and the various parts of the institutions, the various practices within the institutions, often have functions that are not readily or obviously apparent to us. In that sense, they are often latent, and we don't become aware of the linkages and the functions of institutions until we damage them and destroy them.

And so Burke thought that radical reform was based on overrating the extent to which we could understand existing institutions. Plus, he thought, the attempt to subject all institutions to rational scrutiny could have negative consequences of its own, because that could destroy the legitimacy of existing institutions if people came to believe that they didn't hold up to the proper standards of reason without necessarily being able to provide workable alternative institutions.

Edmund Burke was deeply interested in political economy. In fact, he was consulted by Adam Smith when Smith was writing *The Wealth of Nations*. There was a substantial degree of agreement between Burke and Smith about self-interest as an engine of public utility, about the potential benefits of the market and the desirability of free international trade. But Burke was, to a greater extent than Smith, a defender of the aristocracy in the commercial society. His argument was that commercial society tends to be dynamic, quickly changeable, and that the aristocracy provides a kind of anchor, slowing down the pace of historical change so that some of the radical effects of quick, radical historical change could be slowed down and hence ameliorated by having this kind of anchor of the aristocracy.

Burke thought that those people who engaged in commerce—merchants, entrepreneurs, men of money—people who were of more modest backgrounds had more to gain from change, and hence they're more likely to engage in change and to welcome change without the proper degree of caution, because too rapid a change of institutions would have a negative effect.

Burke did have a dynamic view of commercial society. He was well aware that things were changing, and his theory was that as new interests arose, as new economic groups arose, they ought to be represented in the political system. So, he was in favor of the incorporation of new groups with money into the political system and didn't want to maintain a stranglehold by the aristocracy, but he wanted the aristocracy to be there as an anchor and to absorb these new, more dynamic groups. But he was suspicious of too large a role for these new-moneyed men who he thought often didn't have an efficient enough sense of tradition. Burke was also a defender, on similar grounds, of the established church—that is, the Church of England—as a repository of inherited culture.

As a member of Parliament, Burke became a leading critic of the British East India Company. Indeed, before his writings on the French Revolution, that was the role in which he was best known in British political life. In 1756, the British East India Company's headquarters at Calcutta had been attacked by a local Indian ruler. In order to protect its investment and in order to be able to continue to trade in India, the company began a campaign of military conquests that soon left much of Bengal under the company's control.

Burke argued that the company's agents in India were men who had come out of nowhere, of no established position in British life. That's why they went all the way to India. They had come there seeking to strike it rich, and seeking to strike it rich quickly. In their efforts to strike it rich quickly, they were unrestrained by the inherited culture of England, and because they were unrestrained by traditional cultural codes, Burke argued, they were willing to do anything to get rich. He argued that they were riding roughshod over traditional Indian society in their attempt to get rich quickly.

Then, Burke showed, and there was something to this, these new men of the British East India Company, who had come out of nowhere, gotten rich in India, then used their wealth—the wealth that they had acquired through ill-gotten means in India—to buy influence in Parliament, and they used that influence to prevent parliamentary scrutiny of their actions. Burke devoted himself for years to criticizing, scrutinizing, and trying to prosecute what he saw as the evils and crimes committed by representatives of the British East India Company in the course of their commercial life. And from this, Burke seems to have concluded that commerce, when it's unchecked by traditional moral codes, could have negative consequences and, indeed, could erode the foundations of the political order. He saw these men of money as having destroyed the traditional political hierarchy and social hierarchy of India, and now he saw them having a pernicious effect on British politics as well.

Burke then applied this analysis to the French Revolution in his *Reflections on the Revolution in France*, that seminal work of conservative thought. The book was written early on during the French Revolution.

By late 1789, the revolutionary parliament in France, what was called the National Assembly, had done away with the remnants of feudal dues and had established its control over the government. That left this new revolutionary parliament responsible for the national debt, which the French state had incurred, not least through its wars with England.

Late in 1789, in an attempt to cover the national debt, this revolutionary parliament voted to nationalize the assets of the Catholic Church, which at the time was by far the largest landowner in France. The notion was that they would nationalize these assets, they would sell them off to private individuals, and they would use the money that they had obtained to pay off the national debt—and the state, in turn, promised to take over the obligation to pay the clergy and to maintain the churches.

That was the backdrop against which Burke was writing the *Reflections on the Revolution in France*. It was written at an early stage of the revolution when things seemed to be going pretty well, and it predicted that the revolution would get more and more radical, and more and more murderous. And of course, over time, that is indeed what happened. The revolution did get more radical, and in its most radical stages it took tens, indeed, hundreds of thousands of lives.

In Burke's analysis, this process of radicalization was due to the coming together of two forces. On the one hand, of politicized intellectuals who wanted to remake society according to their abstract theories, like equality before the law, and radicalized intellectuals who wanted to undermine the position of the established Catholic Church and its monopoly on education. As Burke saw it, these intellectuals were supported in the French Parliament by men of money, those people who had made a lot of money as tax farmers, who actually held the national debt, and who wanted to be sure that it was paid off. Burke reasoned that men who made their money through commerce and finance rather than through owning agricultural land had a mentality that made them more open to radical innovation. As he put it:

> The monied interest is in its nature more ready for any adventure; and its possessors more disposed to new enterprises of any kind. Being of a recent acquisition, it falls in more naturally with any novelties. It is therefore the kind of wealth which will be resorted to by all who wish for change.

Burke argued that when such people had an influence on politics, they tended to be insufficiently cautious, because in politics, as in business, they were open to novelty, and that's what he saw happening in the National Assembly—that men of money were playing a larger role there. They wanted to secure their investments in the national debt, and they were also open to arguments for radical change and innovation even if such change was risky. After all, innovation and risk was their specialty. They were, therefore, too open to the entreaties of radical intellectuals, including the antipathy of those intellectuals to the established church.

Burke argued that the intellectuals' attack on the church would lead to a decline of the influence of the church, and he argued that that would lead to an erosion of cultural constraints. This was part of Burke's argument, that inherited cultural codes had come about and had largely been transmitted to the present by the church and by the aristocracy, and that weakening the power of these two groups (of the church and the aristocracy) would create people with more freedom but less self-restraint, and that, he thought, would lead to a kind of political radicalization and to behavior that was barbaric.

Reflections on the Revolution in France seemed, after a few years, to be remarkable in its prescience, and there were a number of intellectuals who rejected its analysis about the necessary direction of radicalization of the revolution when it was first published who thereafter embraced the book when they saw that indeed things took more or less the course that Burke had anticipated. At the time that he wrote it, the revolution was still in its liberal, moderate phase. Within a few years, there was the experience of terror and widespread bloodshed.

Burke's main contribution to the debate over capitalism was his notion that commercial society—capitalist society—may depend upon inherited institutions that restrain people and make their behavior more decent. And his argument was that some of these institutions, like the church, are institutions that capitalism doesn't create and that it might actually help to undermine. And if those institutions were undermined, the result would be to create people who pursued their appetites and their self-interest by riding roughshod over others because they weren't restrained by traditional cultural codes in the way that he saw with the officers of the East India Company in India, and in the way that he thought would occur in the course of the French Revolution.

Burke also wrote powerfully about the danger of taking contractual relations as the model of all relations. Contractual relations are the typical relations in the market, and Burke thought that there was a spillover effect of these kinds of relations characteristic of the market on nonmarket relations as well. That was one of his main concerns, and indeed it would be one of the main concerns of conservatives over the decades and, indeed, over the centuries, and that is the spillover effects of the kinds of behaviors and mentalities that are legitimate in the market but might be counterproductive if they spilled beyond the market.

Burke pointed to the importance in some areas of life of noncontractual obligations, and that applied, he thought, to the state. He wrote:

> The state ought not to be considered as nothing better than a partnership agreement in a trade of pepper and coffee, calico or tobacco, or some other such low concern, to be taken up for a little temporary interest, and to be dissolved by the fancy of the parties. ... As the ends of such a partnership cannot be obtained in many generations, it becomes a partnership not only between those who are living, but between those who are living, those who are dead, and those who are to be born.

Or, as Burke put it in another essay published shortly after his *Reflections on the Revolution in France*, he wrote:

> Men without their choice derive benefits from that association [that is, from the state]; without their choice they are subjected to duties in consequence of these benefits; and without their choice they enter into a virtual obligation as binding as any that is actual.

What Burke is saying here, then, is that not everything is a matter of choice, that not every relationship is like a market-oriented contract which one enters into through choice and which one can get out of when one thinks it's no longer in one's interest. There are political institutions. There are, Burke would say, social institutions like the family that can't be accounted for entirely in terms of this logic of free individual choice.

So Burke feared that forces that were unleashed by capitalism, when combined with critical intellectuals who didn't recognize the limits of their own knowledge, could lead to the decline of the inherited institutions that gave life meaning and that restrained people's more harmful urges.

As we'll see, conservatives have been echoing his complaint ever since.

Lecture Twelve
Conservatism and Periphery Capitalism—Möser

Scope:

While Edmund Burke was a conservative in an already commercialized society, his German contemporary Justus Möser (1720–1794) provides an example of a conservative in a precommercial society, for whom the spread of international capitalism was a threat to existing institutions. Möser came from the tiny state of Osnabrück in Westphalia, on the edge of the international capitalist economy. He saw himself as the defender of a traditional, hierarchical society in which people knew their place. His conservatism is reflected in the values that he championed: localism, particularity, historical institutions, hierarchy, limits, and boundaries. For Möser, the influx of new and cheaper goods from abroad, sold through new forms of marketing, was destroying the traditional economy, society, and local culture of his beloved homeland. He thus became an early critic of what later came to be called "globalization."

Outline

I. Justus Möser provides us with an interesting example of a conservative in a precommercial society, a society on the periphery of capitalist development that was being transformed by capitalism in ways that threatened its traditional way of life.

   A. As you'll see, Möser was in many ways a precursor of contemporary critics of what we now call "globalization."

   B. Möser was born and lived most of his life in Osnabrück, in western Germany.

   C. He served for much of his life as the chief administrator of this tiny state of Osnabrück, but he also published articles in newspapers, magazines, and books, so he was part of the print culture of public debate that was such an important element of the Enlightenment.

II. Like Edmund Burke, Möser was a conservative, but the society that he wanted to conserve was a precommercial one.

   A. For Möser, the international market was pernicious because it was destroying the particular local culture of Osnabrück.

- B. The international capitalist economy did so, first, by creating new wants that could not be fulfilled by the traditional economy of the region.
- C. Second, through competition from commodities that could be produced more cheaply abroad, the capitalist market was destroying the traditional guild-based modes of production and the social and political structures with which they were intertwined.
- D. In the subsequent development of capitalism, this fear that local cultures and social structures faced destruction by competition from goods from abroad would often be repeated.

III. The enlightened German political writers of Möser's day regarded the market as a tool that encouraged economic growth.
- A. The state and its citizens, they reasoned, could become richer if men were allowed to follow their "natural" self-interest.
- B. Like Adam Smith, they believed that the task of law was to create the conditions of free competition that would allow the economy to grow.
- C. They urged the monarchs and their bureaucracies to do away with traditional institutions that restricted the sale of land, movement of labor, and entry into occupations. In short, they favored laws that would provide greater legal equality.
- D. Creating such conditions meant doing away with many existing historical institutions.

IV. The society that Möser defended was a corporate society of ranks (*Ständestaat*).
- A. In such a society, property was not private. It was linked to power, which included the control that landowners were able to exert over their serfs.
- B. Nobles, serfs, and independent peasants lived their lives barely aware of the market economy.
- C. The town economy was organized into guilds of artisans, each of which had a monopoly over production and marketing of the commodities it produced.

- **D.** In such a society, status was inherited, not achieved. It was a society oriented toward stability, not growth or dynamism. Social relations were based on deference and paternalism.
- **E.** According to Möser, one advantage of such a society was that everyone knew their place in the social order.

V. In contrast to the Enlightenment's typical emphasis on individual opportunity and autonomy, Möser valued those institutions that circumscribed the individual, if in doing so they provided a firm sense of identity.
- **A.** Experience, he said, embodied a wisdom that general theories of justice and efficiency just couldn't match, because the wisdom of experience took into account that the functions of existing institutions were interlinked.
- **B.** Because institutions were interlinked, reforming one institution might have destructive effects on other institutions, so Möser often saw his role as a conservative intellectual as making explicit the tacit wisdom of existing institutions and practices.
- **C.** Möser scandalized enlightened intellectuals of his day by defending the institution of serfdom, that traditional paternalistic relationship between the lord and serf in which the serf was the lord's legal property.

VI. The traditional society of Osnabrück was being transformed by the spread of capitalism in a number of ways that alarmed Möser.
- **A.** The artisan was central to Osnabrück's political institutions as Möser thought of them, but their status was now being undermined by the international market and its local agents, namely the shopkeeper and the peddler.
- **B.** Möser recognized that the products produced abroad by the method of simplification were often better and less expensive, but he regarded shopkeepers as agents of social destruction.
- **C.** Imported goods had another quality that disturbed Möser, and that was their novelty. For Möser the whole notion of fashion was pernicious because it was at odds with the traditional products created by the guildsmen.

D. He reserved his greatest hostility for the peddler, who was the agent of the market economy in the countryside. To Möser, the activities of the peddlers were ruining the good morals of the rural population by awakening new needs and desires.
   E. Möser also saw the market and its agents as despoiling morals because the market (in the form of the peddler) drew women away from the protected confines of the household and the supervision of their husbands.
VII. Möser also worried about the rise of cottage industry, which provided a new way of making a living but had some destabilizing social effects.
   A. Previously, the population among the peasantry had been quite stable because men and women deferred marriage until they inherited land and could support a family.
   B. Now, there was the ability to earn additional income through cottage industry, and this was leading to earlier marriage and higher fertility.
   C. A whole new class of people was coming into existence, people who were outside the existing social structure and its social hierarchy. They were multiplying more quickly than the economy of the town could absorb them, leading to the issue of pauperism.
   D. Möser analyzed and eloquently expressed the recurrent laments of those who saw their traditional way of life destroyed by the spread of capitalism.

Suggested Reading:

Muller, *Conservatism* (Möser, "On the Diminished Disgrace of Whores and Their Children in Our Day" and "No Promotion According to Merit").

———, *The Mind and the Market*, chap. 4.

Walker, *German Home Towns*, chaps. 1–5.

Questions to Consider:

1. What are the major similarities and differences between the thoughts of Justus Möser and Edmund Burke?
2. What are the advantages and disadvantages of living in the sort of society Möser defended?
3. Do Möser's laments have any contemporary counterparts?

Lecture Twelve—Transcript
Conservatism and Periphery Capitalism—Möser

For Voltaire and for Adam Smith, capitalism was a way of bridging differences between cultures and between societies, but to others the spread of the market looked like a threat to the very existence of their culture and their society. One of those was Justus Möser, who lived from 1720 to 1794, which made him a contemporary of Adam Smith and of Edmund Burke.

Möser provides us with an interesting example of a conservative in a precommercial society, a society on the periphery of capitalist development, a society that was being transformed by capitalism in ways that threatened the traditional way of life of that society. As you'll see, Möser was, in many ways, a precursor of contemporary critics of what we now call "globalization." One of the ongoing motifs of that criticism is the notion that the spread of international capitalism undermines the economic basis of existing communities and societies.

Möser was born and lived most of his life in Osnabrück, which was a small state, really just a town and its hinterland—an area of less than 50 square miles—with about 125,000 inhabitants. It lies in western Germany, not very far from the Dutch border. This was one of the 300 states into which German-speaking Europe was divided before the era of the French Revolution.

Möser came from a family of lawyers and town administrators. He was also a lawyer by training, and he served for much of his life as the chief administrator of Osnabrück. Indeed, from the age of 24 until almost his death in 1794, he was the central political figure in this tiny state. But he was also an author, who published articles on a wide range of contemporary public issues in newspapers and in magazines. These articles were collected and published between hard covers in 1775 under the title *Patriotic Fantasies*, although perhaps a better translation of the title would be "The Local Imagination," for that was the nature of the society that Möser was trying to protect, a local one.

In that he contributed to newspapers and magazines and books, Möser was part of that print culture of public debate that was such an important element of the Enlightenment. Indeed, Möser sometimes debated with himself. In an attempt to reach a wide audience, he would often publish two or three articles with differing perspectives on the same issue, such as, should peddlers be permitted in Osnabrück? Each article was written in the voice of a protagonist, often an enlightened reformer on one hand and a supposedly more down-to-earth conservative critic of the reforms on the other. Usually, though not always, the conservative argument was presented as more convincing. In any case, Möser's significance for us lies in the way in which he provided an articulate voice of cautionary, conservative views within the German Enlightenment.

Like Edmund Burke, Möser was a conservative, but the society that he wanted to conserve was a precommercial one. The political and economic institutions of Osnabrück that Möser defended in his writings were medieval in origin and feudal in their conception. That institutional world was in the process of being destabilized by the solvent of the market economy.

For Justus Möser, the international market was pernicious because it was destroying the particular local culture of Osnabrück; that is to say, it was destroying what made life in Osnabrück unique and special. The international capitalist economy did so, first by creating new wants that couldn't be fulfilled by the traditional economy of the region; and second, as we'll see, it was destroying the traditional guild-based modes of production and the social and political structures that were intertwined with that guild-based production. It was destroying these through competition from commodities that could be produced more cheaply abroad. In the subsequent development of capitalism, this fear would often be repeated—that local cultures and social structures faced destruction by competition from goods from abroad.

The enlightened German political writers of Möser's day regarded the market as a tool that encouraged economic growth, something they were very eager to foster. The state and its citizens, they reasoned, could become richer if men were allowed to follow their "natural" self-interest, as they called it. Like Adam Smith, they believed that the task of the law was to create the conditions of free competition that would allow the economy to grow. So they urged the monarchs and their bureaucracies to do away with traditional institutions that restricted the sale of land, the movement of labor, and entry into occupations. In short, they wanted laws that would provide greater legal equality. That would create the conditions for a more economically dynamic society, but creating those conditions meant doing away with many existing historical institutions.

The society that Möser defended was a hierarchical, corporate society of ranks, what is called in Germany *Ständestaat*. In such a society, property wasn't private. It was linked to power, and that power included the control that noble landowners were able to exert over their serfs.

Since medieval times, the residents of the countryside had been made up of a handful of noble lords and a mass of serfs, along with some peasants who supported themselves by farming. The nobles owned most of the farmable land in the state of Osnabrück. They lived on their rural estates; they derived much of their income from feudal dues that were paid by the serfs, or from the rents that were paid by legally independent peasants. In a society like that, it was considered unsuitable for a noble to work as hard as a commoner, or as long as a commoner, or for the same pay as a commoner. And unlike the commoner, the noble was exempt from taxation. So it was a whole way of life that was distinguished from commoners'.

The lord's holdings were passed on to his descendants and couldn't be bought and sold. The serf wasn't free to own land and couldn't move without the permission of his lord. The free peasants were not serfs, but they typically acquired their land through hereditary leasehold. In other words, they inherited the lease from their parents.

Nobles, serfs, and independent peasants lived their lives barely aware of the market economy. Of course, the market, in the sense of the exchange of goods mediated by money, had played some role even in this traditional society of Osnabrück. But for most lords or serfs or peasants or artisans, the market was marginal to their existence.

The peasant household produced much of what it consumed, and consumed most of what it produced. From time to time, the peasant went to the town market to sell excess eggs, butter, poultry, vegetables that they had grown and to use the money to buy some of the products of the artisans of the town. Those artisans sold what they themselves produced, usually without the intermediary of a merchant or a shopkeeper. So merchants and their commodities had traditionally played a small, marginal role in the life of Osnabrück.

The town economy was organized into guilds of artisans. There were separate guilds for blacksmiths, cobblers, bakers, tanners, butchers, carpenters, cloth makers, and so on. Each guild had a monopoly of production and marketing of the commodities that it produced. Guild regulations specified the conditions under which new people could be accepted into the guild—new apprentices—including provisions that they be of good character and of honorable birth.

After years of working with a guild master, the apprentice eventually moved up to become a journeyman, and eventually rose to become a master himself after demonstrating his skill by producing a masterpiece. The political representation of members of the guild was through the guild itself. Each guild elected a guild master, who represented the members of the guild on the town council. The policies of the guilds, and of the town councils that they dominated, was to restrict admission into their trades and to press for exclusive rights to sell their products in the town and the surrounding countryside. Each guild had the right to enforce its monopoly by confiscating products that came in from outside the town and that the guild itself produced. As in other parts of Osnabrück society, what a man's parents had been largely determined his own vocation. In admitting new apprentices, the sons of masters were given advantages.

In a society like this, status was inherited; it wasn't achieved. It was a society oriented toward stability, not to growth or dynamism. Social relations were based on deference and paternalism. Deference—that is, you were supposed to look up to those above you in the social hierarchy. Paternalism—you were supposed to look out for those below you in the social hierarchy.

According to Möser, one advantage of such a society was that everyone knew their place in the social order. In Möser's view, a person acquired his identity from his place in the institutional structure of society, a society in which economic, social, and political institutions weren't distinguished from one another. A person's status as a guildsman or a noble landowner or a serf or an independent peasant determined not only how he earned his living but his sense of who he was, of what his duties and obligations were, of those to whom he ought to defer, and those who ought to defer to him.

Möser's defense of such a society emphasized the benefits of knowing one's place, the importance of belonging to an existing collectivity, and therefore the need to cultivate loyalty to existing institutions because they provided the individual with a firm sense of place.

In contrast to the Enlightenment's typical emphasis on individual opportunity and individual autonomy, Möser valued those institutions that circumscribed the individual, that surrounded him, if in doing so they provided a firm sense of identity. And so what conservatives saw as stability, enlighteners saw as stagnation. What conservatives like Möser saw as institutions that gave men a sense of identity, gave men a sense of being part of a world of clearly defined markers, enlightened bureaucrats saw as limiting opportunity and limiting individual creativity.

"Our ancestors," Möser wrote, "were guided by experience rather than by theories." And this contrast between experience and theory was often repeated by Möser and became a staple of later conservative thought. Experience, it was said, embodied a wisdom which general theories of justice and efficiency just couldn't match, because the wisdom of experience took into account that the functions of existing institutions were interlinked, that guilds, for example, were interlinked with familial institutions because if you were a member of the guild and you got sick or you died, the guild would look after other members of your family. And because institutions were interlinked, reforming one institution might have destructive effects on other institutions, so Möser often saw his role as a conservative intellectual as discovering and making explicit the tacit wisdom of existing institutions and practices.

Möser scandalized enlightened intellectuals of his day by defending the institution of serfdom, that traditional paternalistic relationship between the lord and serf, in which the serf was the lord's legal property. In fact, Möser claimed, serfdom as it actually existed in Westphalia was superior to economic relationships based upon the legal freedom of both partners, that is, the Enlightenment ideal. He argued that once the serf had redeemed himself by buying his legal freedom through a cash payment to the lord, the lord ended up losing all interest in the serf and his welfare. Möser writes that a serf is like a horse that is owned by a carriage driver. Since the carriage driver owns the horse permanently, it's in the owner's interest to look after the horse and maintain him in good condition. But a peasant farmer who rents his land from a landowner is like a rented horse, which one exploits as much as possible without concern for his future welfare. By the way, similar arguments were made in the antebellum American South regarding the supposed advantages of slavery over free labor on precisely these grounds.

But the traditional society of Osnabrück was being transformed by the spread of capitalism in a number of ways that alarmed Möser. The artisan was central to Osnabrück's political institutions as Möser thought of them. He was the one who paid taxes. He was the one who could be called upon in times of war to provide quarter for professional soldiers. He was the one that provided traditional products to meet the customary needs of the people of the region. So as Möser saw it, economic privileges, the monopoly that the artisanal guilds had, and their political duties were neatly intertwined within a stable economy. But the status of these guilded artisans, Möser believed, was now being undermined by the international market and its local agents, namely the shopkeeper and the peddler.

The shopkeeper imported goods from outside of Osnabrück and sold them in his shop. These goods came from London, Paris, from big cities in Germany, where they were produced by a process that Möser called "simplification," by which he meant that process of manufacture represented by Adam Smith's pin factory, where in place of the guilded master artisan who worked with a few apprentices, this new style of production involved a master who employed 30 or 40 wage laborers. The process of production was broken down into steps, each of which was performed by a worker who specialized in that phase, as opposed to the traditional artisanal mode of production where the master artisan would know how to make the whole thing.

Möser recognized that the products produced by this method were often better, and certainly less expensive, than those produced by the hometown artisans. But Möser regarded the shopkeepers who imported and sold these goods as agents of social destruction because by importing cheaper and more desirable goods from abroad, they were undermining that artisanal guild economy on which the town's culture and political institutions had rested.

And so, Möser said, the artisan was increasingly being displaced by the shopkeeper. He estimated that in the last century the number of artisans in Osnabrück had fallen by about half, while the number of shopkeepers had tripled, from a very low base, of course. So the independent artisanry was in economic decline, and with it, the urban institutions of the corporate society of Osnabrück.

Imported goods had another quality that disturbed Möser, and that was their novelty. He writes that in the great cities, tastes and styles are constantly changing, while the town artisan makes his goods in the traditional way. So for Möser the whole notion of fashion was pernicious because it was at odds with the traditional products created by the guildsmen.

The shopkeeper thrived by encouraging the taste for fashion and for luxury, that is to say, by stimulating new desires. The Lord's prayer urges, "Lead us not into temptation," but according to Möser that was one of the roles of the shopkeeper, the local agent of the new international economy, who robbed the artisan of his customers and of his livelihood. By encouraging the consumption of foreign goods at the expense of those produced locally, the shopkeeper enriched foreigners, according to Möser, while impoverishing his fellow citizens.

The complaint that the lower classes were buying goods that were inappropriate for their station in life was a constant lament among 18th-century conservatives, and Möser reserved his greatest hostility for the peddler, who as he saw it, and quite rightly, was the agent of the market economy in the countryside.

In the primitive economy of rural Westphalia, peasants had very few opportunities to encounter goods that were made abroad. The roads were poor, and that made it difficult and hazardous to travel, so the peasants rarely visited the town and its shops. Fairs at which foreign goods might be purchased were few and far between.

In such economically backward regions, the main source of foreign goods was the peddler, a man who carried his stocks on his back and marched off through the paths and byways to the homes of the peasants. Peddlers are very interesting figures in the history of capitalism. They're really the cutting edge of the spread of the capitalist market.

The peasants didn't seem to most people like a very promising market. They had little to spend, and they were hard to reach, but to the peddler, a would-be merchant with little capital and no inherited status, the peasants represented an untapped market. So the peddler carried items produced outside the region and sold them in small quantities to people like the peasants who were largely outside the market economy.

To Möser, the activities of the peddlers were ruining the good morals, as he called them, of the rural population by awakening new needs and new desires. Once, Möser claimed, the peasants had been satisfied with local products, and they didn't aspire to foreign-made goods that were above their station. It was the peddler who led them astray by encouraging them to buy items they would never have thought about on their own. The peddler led people to buy what Möser thought they didn't really need. What they did need, Möser assumed, was what they had traditionally needed. As Möser saw it, it was the aim of government policymakers like himself to protect the public from the temptation of buying products that Möser knew they didn't really need.

This lament that people are buying things that they don't really need has been a recurrent one in the history of capitalism. We've already seen it going back to the debate over luxury that we've already examined, and this lament extends into the present.

As we'll see, there may be something to this lament. It's not a claim that we should dismiss lightly, but in view of this ongoing condemnation of people for buying things that the observer knows they don't really need, it's interesting to look at the products that Möser was sure the peasants didn't really need. What were these pernicious, but tempting, goods to which the peddler exposed unsuspecting peasants and their wives? Silk kerchiefs, linen, leather gloves, wool stockings, metal buttons, mirrors, cotton caps, knives, and needles. These are the sorts of things that the defenders of customary consumption regarded as luxuries, but it's easy to imagine that such goods simply increased the quality of life of the peasants who purchased them, making life a little bit easier, or a bit more comfortable, or a bit more colorful.

Möser also saw the market and its agents as despoiling morals because, he argued, the market (in the form of the peddler) drew women away from the protected confines of the household and the supervision of their husbands. The peddler, after all, appeared at the peasant's door, and if the person there was the housewife, to whom the peddler was trying to sell his goods, then she was unprotected by the protective influence of her husband.

Here, too, Möser was a precursor of an ongoing accusation that the market comes to permeate the family, that it attacks the family at its weakest, most defenseless points. And Möser in this case was dismayed by this direct appeal of the peddler to the woman without the steadying presence of her husband. Once again, the market was portrayed as the destroyer of custom and tradition.

Möser also worried about another capitalist innovation that was actually changing the very structure of Osnabrück society, namely, the rise of cottage industry, which provided a new way of making a living with some destabilizing social effects. Previously, the population among the peasantry had been quite stable, because men and women deferred marriage until they inherited land and could support a family, and they usually inherited land when their parents were old or sick or dead. So men typically didn't marry until about the age of 30, when they inherited the family plot, and women were not too much younger. That left a relatively limited number of years of fertility, and so it limited the number of children that they produced.

Now, there was the ability to earn additional income through cottage industry, and it was leading to earlier marriage and a higher fertility. Many residents of Osnabrück became more closely tied to the growing international market economy through the spread of rural home-based manufacture, what was sometimes called "cottage industry," or the "putting-out system." Under this system, cloth was produced in steps by peasants in their cottages. Within their homes, some peasants would spin, others would weave, others would dye, and others would sew the resulting cloth. The system was created and it was held together by merchants who advanced the peasants the raw material, and often the necessary equipment, and the merchant would move the product on through the various steps and, finally, market the finished product.

In some parts of Europe, and Möser's Osnabrück was among them, this growth of cottage industry was creating a rapid rise in population. Möser was very aware of the impact of these new economic opportunities on the society of Osnabrück, and the social effects of these new economic patterns worried him because, he said, once a man could earn a living through cottage industry, he didn't have to wait to inherit the farm. He could afford to marry at 20, and under those conditions there were much higher levels of fertility. The rate of population growth among these people was a third higher than among the traditional peasants who simply worked on their own land. And so a whole new class of people was coming into existence, people who were outside the existing social structure and its social hierarchy. They weren't lords, they weren't serfs, they weren't peasants, they weren't artisans. They didn't fit in, and they were multiplying more quickly than the economy of the town could absorb them, leading to the issue of pauperism.

Justus Möser analyzed and eloquently expressed the recurrent laments of those who see their traditional way of life destroyed by the spread of capitalism. He was among the first to state a dilemma that we'll find in many future critics of the cultural effects of the rise of the market. It was leading to new forms of production, and new forms of retailing that were destroying traditional occupations. It was leading to changes in social structure that came about as a result of the new ways of making a living. It was leading to the creation of new wants and new needs that were fostered by entrepreneurs, by shopkeepers, by peddlers. Anxiety about the effects of the market was to become the most consistent theme within conservative social and political thought.

To Möser, the idea of a society in which everyone knew his place sounded attractive, where you knew what your duties were, you knew what your responsibilities were, you knew that the political institutions of society were there to protect your traditional way of life. No doubt it sounds attractive to some of us as well. But who of us would rather live in Möser's world, with its fixed hierarchies determined largely by birth, its routine, and its limited material horizons?

Was there a way of reconciling the institutions of the market with the sense of identity that Möser so valued in precapitalist Germany? That was the issue to which Hegel would turn his attention in the next generation, the generation after the French Revolution.

Timeline

B.C.

384–322	Life of Aristotle.

A.D.

354–430	Life of Augustine of Hippo.
1139	Usury expressly forbidden by the second Lateran Council.
1225–1286	Life of Thomas Aquinas.
1600	British East India Company granted royal charter for monopoly on trade with India.
1602	Founding of the Amsterdam Stock Exchange and of the Dutch East India Company, the first company to issue public stock.
1609	Bank of Amsterdam founded.
1651	Thomas Hobbes's *Leviathan, or the Matter, Forme, and Power of a Common-wealth Ecclesiasticall and Civill*.
1662	Pieter de la Court's *The True Interest and Political Maxims of the Republic of Holland*.
1675	Pierre Nicole's "Of Charity and Self-Love."
1689	John Locke's *Two Treatises of Government*.
1694	Bank of England founded, a key development in the financial revolution.
1706	Bernard Mandeville's *The Fable of the Bees*.

1707	Act of Union joins England and Scotland into Great Britain.
1711	*The Spectator*, the first journal of public opinion, is founded in England with the aim of bringing "philosophy out of closets and libraries, to dwell in clubs and assemblies."
1734	Voltaire's *Letters on England*.
1736	Voltaire's "The Worldling."
1750	Jean-Jacques Rousseau's "Discourse on the Arts and Sciences."
1755	Jean-Jacques Rousseau's "Discourse on the Origin and Foundations of Inequality among Men."
1759	Adam Smith's *The Theory of Moral Sentiments*.
1762	Jean-Jacques Rousseau's *The Social Contract*.
1765	Josiah Wedgwood opens first showroom in London, a key development of the consumer revolution of the 18th century.
1769	Voltaire's *Philosophical Dictionary*.
1775	Justus Möser's *Patriotic Fantasies*.
1776	James Watt's steam engine installed for commercial use; Adam Smith's *An Inquiry into the Nature and Causes of the Wealth of Nations*.
1783	Edmund Burke's *Ninth Report of the Select Committee on India*.
1789	French Revolution begins.
1790	Edmund Burke's *Reflections on the Revolution in France*.

1791	Alexander Hamilton's *Report on the Subject of Manufactures*; first Bank of the U.S. chartered.
1820	G. W. F. Hegel's *The Philosophy of Right*.
1824	Henry Clay outlines the "American System" of protection.
1827	Friedrich List's *Outlines of American Political Economy*.
1828	Protectionist tariff on import of manufactured goods passed by U.S. Congress, in part due to influence of List's book, and leading to Southern protest against "The Tariff of Abominations."
1830	First British railway built.
1835–1840	Alexis de Tocqueville's *Democracy in America*.
1845	Friedrich Engels's *The Condition of the Working Class in England*.
1847	Founding of the first Siemens company.
1848	Karl Marx and Friedrich Engels's *The Communist Manifesto*; failed revolutions in continental Europe.
1855	Limited Liability Act (UK).
1863	Limited liability law adopted in France.
1864	Founding of International Workingmen's Association, in which Marx soon became active.
1867	Karl Marx's *Capital*, vol. 1.
1870	Deutsche Bank formed.

1871	Trade Union Act (UK) gives legal protection to unions; unification of Germany; Thyssen and Co. founded.
1887	Ferdinand Tönnies's *Community and Society*.
1900	Georg Simmel's *The Philosophy of Money*.
1902	Werner Sombart's *Modern Capitalism* (vols. 1 and 2); John A. Hobson's *Imperialism*; V. I. Lenin's *What Is to Be Done?*
1903	Werner Sombart's *The German Economy in the Nineteenth Century*; Ford Motor Co. established.
1904–1905	Max Weber's *The Protestant Ethic and the "Spirit" of Capitalism*.
1908	General Motors founded; Henry Ford introduces the Model T.
1910	Rudolf Hilferding's *Finance Capital*.
1911	Joseph Schumpeter's *The Theory of Economic Development*.
1913	Federal Reserve System established in U.S.; Rosa Luxembourg's *The Accumulation of Capital: A Contribution to an Economic Analysis of Imperialism*.
1914–1918	World War I.
1916	V. I. Lenin's *Imperialism: The Highest Stage of Capitalism*.
1917	Bolshevik Revolution in Russia.
1918	Joseph Schumpeter's "The Sociology of Imperialism."

1918–1919	Abortive communist revolutions in Berlin, Budapest, and Vienna.
1920	Ludwig von Mises's *Economic Calculation in the Socialist Commonwealth*.
1923	Max Weber's *Economy and Society*; Carl Schmitt's *The Crisis of Parliamentary Democracy*.
1924	Ford produces 10 millionth car.
1928	First Soviet Five-Year Plan.
1929	Crash of New York Stock Exchange.
1930	Parliamentary crisis in Germany leads to suspension of parliamentary government; large electoral gains by National Socialists and Communists.
1931	Hans Freyer's *Revolution from the Right*; Carl Schmitt's *The Protector of the Constitution*.
1932	Franklin D. Roosevelt elected president in U.S.
1933	National Socialists come to power in Germany; Franklin D. Roosevelt inaugurated in U.S.; National Recovery Administration created.
1935	Sidney and Beatrice Webb's *Soviet Communism: A new civilization?*; Friedrich von Hayek's *Collectivist Economic Planning*; Social Security Act (U.S.) instituted.
1936	John Maynard Keynes's *The General Theory of Employment, Interest, and Money*.
1939–1945	World War II.

1942	Richard and Kathleen Titmuss's *Parents Revolt—A Study of Declining Birthrates in Acquisitive Societies*; Sir William Beveridge's *Report of the Inter-Departmental Committee on Social Insurance and Allied Services*; Jospeh Schumpeter's *Capitalism, Socialism and Democracy*.
1944	Friedrich von Hayek, *The Road to Serfdom*.
1945	Election of Labour government in Britain.
1947	Beginning of the Marshall Plan (European Recovery Program).
1950	IBM begins producing computers.
1956	C. A. R. Crosland's *The Future of Socialism*.
1964	Herbert Marcuse's *One-Dimensional Man*.
1965	Mancur Olson's *The Logic of Collective Action: Public Goods and the Theory of Groups*.
1973	Daniel Bell's *The Coming of Post-Industrial Society: A Venture in Social Forecasting*.
1976	Daniel Bell's *The Cultural Contradictions of Capitalism*; Friedrich von Hayek's *The Mirage of Social Justice*.
1978	Beginning of economic reform in the People's Republic of China.
1979	Margaret Thatcher becomes British prime minister.
1981	IBM personal computer announced.

1983 ....Ernest Gellner's *Nations and Nationalism*.

1986 ....Mikhail Gorbachev initiates policy of perestroika (reform) in U.S.S.R.

1989 ....Fall of the Berlin Wall; effective end of communism in Europe.

1991 ....Dissolution of Soviet Union.

Glossary

civil society: Hegel used the term to refer to the realm between the family and the state, which he saw as characteristic of modernity. Its major institution was the market. More recent thinkers have tended to use the term in a more Tocquevillian sense, to refer to voluntary associations that are not part of the family, market, or state.

commercial society: Adam Smith's term for a society constituted by the market and by government capable of enforcing the rule of law.

commodification: The process by which goods previously produced directly are instead purchased.

commodity: An item or service that is bought and sold in the market.

consumer revolution: The history of capitalism is the history of consumption. While historians have discovered consumer revolutions going back to at least the 17th century, the term is conventionally used for the expansion of consumer goods and marketing in Britain in the second half of the 18th century.

corporate society (German: *Ständestaat*): A social and political system, characteristic of much of early modern continental Europe, in which society is organized into a hierarchy of legally recognized corporate groups (estates) with different rights and privileges, such as the clergy, nobility, citizens of towns, and serfs.

false consciousness: The Marxist doctrine that workers may fail to pursue their collective self-interest of embracing socialism because they have been conned by some nefarious force.

fascism: A 20th-century political ideology that stresses strong hierarchical leadership, a powerful state, and national self-assertion, while eschewing liberalism and democracy.

guild: An association of producers of some service or commodity, with a legally recognized monopoly and exclusive criteria of membership. Guilds dominated urban economic life in much of continental Europe until the era of the French Revolution.

horizontal integration: The process by which a company expands through developing or acquiring related product lines.

imperialism: Properly, the political control of one polity by another. Often extended promiscuously to include the economic domination of one polity over another.

invisible hand: Adam Smith's metaphor for the unintended socially positive effects of self-interested action, when the institutional structure channels self-interest in socially desirable directions.

laissez-faire: A popular synonym for "free market economics," drawn from the maxim of the French physiocrats, "*Laissez-faire, laissez-passer*," ("let it be," or "leave it alone"), eschewing government interference with trade. Often attributed to Adam Smith, especially by those who haven't read him.

limited liability corporation: The legal restriction of an owner's loss in a business to the amount of capital he has invested in it. Before legislation permitting such bodies in the second half of the 19th century, in case of bankruptcy, investors could be made liable for full debt of the corporation. The limitation of this liability provided an incentive to invest and radically increased the capital available for investment.

Marshall Plan (European Recovery Program): An American government program, begun in 1948, that channeled funds for investment to the capital-deprived nations of Western Europe, which used it to restore infrastructure, import capital goods and jump-start their economies. The Organization for European Economic Cooperation, created to channel the funds, evolved into the Organization of Economic Cooperation and Development (made up of European states, the United States, and Canada), the source of much economic information.

mercantilism: Never a formal doctrine, and named only in retrospect by critics such as Adam Smith, a series of policies in early modern Europe that tried to foster domestic economic growth and subordinated trade to the military needs of the state.

monopoly: Originally, the legal privilege of having the exclusive right to engage in some economic activity. Often used to denote a market for some commodity dominated by a single firm, which is able to obtain higher prices because of a lack of competition.

National Recovery Administration: The NRA allowed industries to create "codes of fair competition," and industry heads to collectively set minimum prices. These were intended to reduce "destructive competition" and to help workers by setting minimum wages and maximum weekly hours. Adopted by Congress in 1933, it was declared unconstitutional by the Supreme Court in 1935.

offshoring: The export of production abroad in search of lower production costs and hence higher profits.

oligopoly: A market that is dominated by a few large suppliers.

outsourcing: Purchasing some service or commodity that had once been made within a firm from an external firm, in order to take advantage of the division of labor, lower costs, and increase profits.

pleonexia: Aristotle's concept of "overreaching" into extremity, wanting ever more, or open-ended desire.

rational ignorance: The theorem of public choice theory that because acquiring the knowledge of government policy required to ascertain the interests of one's group requires time, money, and attention, for those with a small stake in the outcome, it is not worth their while to obtain the necessary knowledge.

"repressive desublimation": Marcuse's contention that contemporary capitalism appeals to direct satisfaction of erotic instincts as a way of controlling the populace and preventing radical change that would bring about a less repressive society.

"self-interest rightly understood": De Tocqueville's phrase for the recognition that it is not in one's self-interest to act egoistically much of the time, leading to the development of habits such as temperance and self-control.

usury: In Catholic thought, the lending of money at (any) interest. In other traditions, the lending of money at excessive interest.

vertical integration: The process by which a company expands by acquiring its suppliers or customers.

welfare state: The term adopted in the United Kingdom to describe the governmental provision of a panoply of social services "from the cradle to the grave." More loosely, the "safety net" of social services provided by the state alongside the capitalist economy.

zero-sum game: A situation in which one can gain only when another loses. Typical of circumstances in which there is no economic growth, or where the objects of desire are relative to one another.

Biographical Notes

Arnold, Matthew (1822–1888): The son of Thomas Arnold, who was the headmaster of the Rugby School for the instruction of "Christian gentlemen," Matthew Arnold became a distinguished poet, social critic, educational theorist, and religious thinker. The best known of his poems, "Dover Beach" (published in 1867), explores the consolations of love amid the decline of traditional religious faith. For much of his life, he earned a living as a government inspector of schools run by the dissenting sects—an object of his critique—that formed the backbone of the British commercial classes. His major works of social criticism, which first appeared in syndicated form in the great Victorian journals and did much to create the social role of critic, include "Democracy" (1861), "The Function of Criticism at the Present Time" (1864), *Culture and Anarchy* (1867–1869), and "Equality" (1878). His volumes of religious thought, which attempted to state the case for a nonsupernatural religion, were highly influential in his day as statements of liberal Christianity, especially *Literature and Dogma* (1873) and *God and the Bible* (1874).

Barbon, Nicholas (c. 1640–1698): Born in London, he studied medicine in Holland, then returned to England, where he was entrepreneurially engaged in rebuilding London after the Great Fire of 1666, helped to create fire insurance, and was active in finance and in politics, serving as a member of Parliament. His *Discourse of Trade* (1690) was among the best-known tracts advocating freedom of trade and exploring the political implications of commerce.

Bell, Daniel (b. 1919): Among the most influential American social scientists of the second half of the 20th century. He began his intellectual life as a journalist, first as managing editor at *The New Leader*, a social democratic magazine (1941–1945), then as labor editor at *Fortune* (1948–1958). He was a Professor of Sociology at Columbia from 1959 to 1969, before moving to Harvard. His collection of essays, *The End of Ideology* (1960; revised edition 1962) explored developments in American society and social thought, as well as the declining plausibility of socialism. In 1965, together with Irving Kristol, he founded *The Public Interest*, a journal devoted to bridging the gap between the academic social sciences and public policy debates. *The Coming of Post-Industrial Society: A Venture in Social Forecasting* (1973) analyzed the shift from an industrial to a knowledge- and service-based economy. *The Cultural Contradictions of Capitalism* (1976) was a work of cultural, social, and political criticism and analysis.

Buchanan, James M. (b. 1919): Among the founders of "public choice theory," which tries to analyze governmental economic actions based on the assumption that politicians and government officials are self-interested actors and tries to suggest constitutional restraints to improve public welfare. His major works include *The Calculus of Consent: Logical Foundations of Constitutional Democracy* (1962), which was written with Gordon Tullock. In 1986 he was awarded the Nobel Prize in Economic Science.

Burke, Edmund (1729–1797): Among the most influential intellectuals in 18th-century political life, Burke became one of the founders of conservatism. Born in Dublin to a Catholic mother and Anglican father, he studied law in London but pursued his career as a man of letters. His first book, a satirical critique of the radical Enlightenment à la Rousseau was published under a pseudonym in 1756 as *A Vindication of Natural Society: A View of the Miseries and Evils Arising to Mankind*. The next year, he published *A Philosophical Enquiry into the Origin of Our Ideas of the Sublime and the Beautiful*, in which he argued that "a consideration of the rationale of our passions seems to me very necessary for all who would affect them upon solid and sure principles." In 1758, Burke launched the *Annual Register*, a survey of the major European political, literary, social, and artistic events of the preceding year. In 1765, he became a member of Parliament, becoming the brain behind the faction of the Whig Party led by his patron, Lord Rockingham. Among the highlights of his parliamentary career were his speeches "On Conciliation with America" (1775), an exploration of American political culture, and "The Nabob of Arcot's Debts" (1785), part of his decade-long attempt to expose the corruption and corrupting effects of the British East India Company. With the outbreak of the French Revolution, he turned his attention to France, and in late 1790 published *Reflections on the Revolution in France*, a seminal work of modern conservatism.

Crosland, C. A. R. (Anthony) (1918–1977): An Oxford don who taught economics, Crosland was a member of Parliament for the British Labour Party from 1950 until he lost his seat in 1955. He then set to work on *The Future of Socialism*, published in late 1956. In

1959 he returned to Parliament, becoming a senior minister in the Labor governments of the 1960s and early 1970s and remaining in office until his death in 1977.

De Tocqueville, Alexis: *See* **Tocqueville, Alexis de.**

Engels, Friedrich (1820–1895): Became a close collaborator of Karl Marx. Born in the Rhineland in western Germany, Engels came from a family of textile manufacturers, with branches in Germany and England. He studied in Berlin, where he associated with the Young Hegelians and was politically radicalized. In 1842, at his family's insistence, he took up a managerial post at the family's business in Manchester, England, then the center of the Industrial Revolution. In 1845 he published his first book, *The Condition of the Working Class in England*, a radical report and critique of the effects of capitalist industrialization on the working class. Engels's essay "Outlines of a Critique of Political Economy," which condemned capitalism on moral grounds as a system founded upon greed, was published by Karl Marx in a short-lived journal that he edited, and deeply influenced Marx's own thinking. The two young radicals wrote a number of works together, culminating in *The Communist Manifesto*. Like Marx, Engels returned to Germany in 1848 to participate in the abortive revolution. Thereafter, he too moved to England, working in the family's business in Manchester, and using the income he earned to support Marx. In 1870 he retired from the business and moved to London; wrote a number of influential works including his critique of the bourgeois family, *The Origin of the Family, Private Property, and the State*; and after Marx's death, edited and published his friend's posthumous works.

Freyer, Hans (1887–1969): A German sociologist, political theorist, and sometime political ideologist. Born to a religious Protestant family, he studied theology and philosophy, participated in the antibourgeois German youth movement, and served as an officer in the First World War. In 1925 he became the first chaired Professor of Sociology at a German university (in Leipzig). Influenced by Hegel, Tönnies, Simmel, Weber, and Oswald Spengler, among others, he developed an antiliberal conception of the state (*Der Staat*, 1925), an activist conception of sociology (*Soziologie als Wirklichkeitswissenschaft*, 1930), and a philosophy of history that saw a powerful national state as the new locus of community. In 1931, he published his political booklet, *Revolution from the Right*, which looked to the nationalist, radical right as the force that would "overcome bourgeois society." He greeted the National Socialist accession to power with hope and collaborated with the regime before eventually becoming disillusioned with it.

Gellner, Ernest (1925–1995): Gellner was raised in a German-speaking Jewish family in Prague. The family emigrated to England in 1939. During the war, Gellner enlisted in the Czech Armoured Brigade, in which capacity he returned briefly to his native city. After studying at Oxford, he went on to a variety of academic posts, first at the London School of Economics, where he taught sociology and philosophy, then in 1984 to Cambridge, where he held the chair in social anthropology. In 1993, he returned to Prague to head the Center for the Study of Nationalism at the Central European University. Gellner's was a wide-ranging mind, and among his works was a study of the fundamental transformations of human history, *Plough, Sword, and Book: The Structure of Human History* (1988). His most important books on nationalism are *Nations and Nationalism* (1983) and *Encounters with Nationalism* (1994).

Hamilton, Alexander (1755–1804): Born on the island of Nevis in the West Indies, to parents who were not legally married. Despite a difficult childhood, his obvious precocity led to his being sent to New Jersey for schooling, and then to King's College (now Columbia University) in New York City. A supporter of the Revolutionary cause, he joined the army and became a leading aide to General George Washington. In 1782 he was elected to Congress, where he worked to create a revenue base that would provide the federal government with real power. Frustrated by what he saw as the dangerous weakness of the federal government, he returned to New York, began a career in law, and founded the Bank of New York in 1784. Three years later, he was a major force at the Constitutional Convention that drafted the American Constitution, then recruited James Madison and John Jay to join him in writing *The Federalist Papers*, defending the need for a strong federal government. That document remains the most important work of American political theory. From 1789 to 1795, Hamilton served as the first secretary of the treasury, under President Washington. During his first two years in office, he presented four seminal reports on economic matters, culminating in his *Report on the Subject of Manufactures* of 1791. Hamilton helped found the United States Mint; helped found the first national bank; and developed a system of duties, tariffs, and excises. In short, he created an apparatus that gave the new government financial stability and gave investors sufficient confidence to invest in government bonds. He died as the result of wounds sustained in a duel with Aaron Burr.

Hansen, Alvin (1887–1975): An influential American economist associated with the New Deal. In 1935 he played a role in the creation of the Social Security system. Appointed Professor of Economics at Harvard University in 1937, he was a leading proponent of the notion that without governmental management of the economy, capitalism was doomed to stagnation—an argument laid out in *Full Recovery or Stagnation?* (1938) and expanded in an article the following year, "Economic Progress and Declining Population Growth." His 1941 book on fiscal policy and business cycles was the first major work in the United States to entirely support Keynes's analysis of the causes of the Great Depression, and he used that analysis to support Keynes's recommendation of the use of deficit spending to stimulate the economy during downturns of the business cycle. Hansen's stagnationist theories were refuted by Schumpeter in *Capitalism, Socialism and Democracy*.

Hayek, Friedrich August von (1899–1992): Born and raised in Vienna in a family of academics and civil servants. He served in the First World War, flirted with reformist socialism, but (deeply influenced by Ludwig von Mises) embraced classical liberalism. As an economist in Vienna, he wrote a stinging critique of the effect of rent control on the Austrian economy, as well as works on monetary theory. In 1931 he became a Professor of Economics at the London School of Economics and a leading critic of Keynes. Appalled by the vogue for governmental planning of the economy, in 1935 he edited and contributed to the volume *Collectivist Economic Planning: Critical Studies on the Possibilities of Socialism*. During the Second World War, while living in Cambridge, he wrote his polemical critique of collectivism, *The Road to Serfdom* (1944). The book made a splash in Britain and even more so in the United States, where an abridged version appeared in the mass-circulation *Reader's Digest*. Not long thereafter he published his seminal essay, "The Use of Knowledge in Society" (perhaps his most important contribution to social science). From 1950 to 1962, Hayek taught at the University of Chicago. It was there that he published his critical, though not entirely hostile, exploration of the welfare state, *The Constitution of Liberty* (1960), a process he continued in the three volumes of *Law, Legislation, and Liberty* (1973–1979). In 1974 he was awarded the Nobel Prize for Economics, jointly with the Swedish socialist Gunner Myrdal. In the age of Thatcher and Reagan, and after the fall of communism in the Soviet bloc, the relevance of Hayek's work on the coordinating function of the market was broadly acknowledged.

Hegel, Georg Wilhelm Friedrich (1770–1831): Born into a family of civil servants and clerics in the Duchy of Württemberg in southwestern Germany. He studied at the Tübinger Stift (a Protestant seminary attached to the university), an institution that incubated many of Germany's leading 19th-century intellectuals, including Friedrich Nietzsche. As a young man, he was deeply influenced by Kant, followed the progress of the French Revolution with sympathy, and was led to reflect upon the reasons for its descent into terror. In 1807 he published *The Phenomenology of Geist* ("mind," or "spirit"), which in a highly abstract manner tried to provide a historical and philosophical account of the development of the human spirit toward an awareness of freedom. In 1818 he was invited by the liberalizing Prussian regime to assume the chair of philosophy at the newly founded University of Berlin. It was there that he published *The Philosophy of Right* in 1820, a sort of précis of his lecture course on the subject. (Student notes of those lectures, since published, have helped to flesh out the text.) The book reflected, among other sources, his reading of Smith's *Wealth of Nations*. Hegel died in the cholera epidemic of 1831.

Hobbes, Thomas (1588–1679): Perhaps the greatest philosopher in the English language, and (together with Spinoza) the progenitor of the Enlightenment. Born to an impecunious family. His intellectual gifts were recognized early, and he was sent to Oxford, where he became a humanist, steeped in the Greek and Latin classics. (In 1629, he published the first translation into English of Thucydides's *History of the Peloponnesian War*.) Like other humanists, he earned a living as a private tutor, secretary, and advisor to the great—in his case to the Cavendish family. Trips to the Continent brought him into contact with leading scientists (including Galileo) and critical philosophers. Hobbes wrote on mathematics, physics, and optics, and in 1642 he published *On the Citizen*, his most important work of political philosophy before *Leviathan*. He became involved in the polarization between the King and Parliament as a defender of royal authority, and fearing for his life in an era of civil war, he fled to

Paris in 1640, where he remained until 1651. It was there that he wrote *Leviathan*, which includes a materialist metaphysics, an exploration of the passions as motivational factors in human action, and an extended critique of the plausibility of revealed religion, as well as the theory of advantages of leaving the anarchic state of nature by forming a state. His work was debated, reviled, and often tacitly accepted while it was explicitly renounced.

Keynes, John Maynard (1883–1946): The most influential British economist of the 20th century. Trained at Cambridge in mathematics, philosophy, and economics, he taught at Cambridge (where he made a fortune for King's College by managing its investments), served in the UK Treasury during the First and Second World Wars, and was a noted commentator on public affairs. His 1919 critique of the Versailles Treaty, *The Economic Consequences of the Peace*, began the process of turning British elite opinion toward greater sympathy with Germany. As a response to ongoing high levels of unemployment in Britain, in 1924 he challenged fiscal orthodoxy by recommending deficit spending on public works to stimulate the sluggish economy in *Does Unemployment Need a Drastic Remedy?* In *A Treatise on Money* (1930), he further departed from fiscal orthodoxy by suggesting that there are economic conditions under which savings do not lead to investment, and that in the midst of an economic depression, the correct course of action should be to encourage spending and discourage saving. His greatest contribution to economic science was *The General Theory of Employment, Interest and Money*, in which he contested the classical economic theory that full employment could always be reached by making wages sufficiently low. Over and above its immediate policy implications, the book suggested fiscal tools for managing the economy and categories of analysis that influenced economic policy and analysis for decades.

Lenin, Vladimir Ilyich (1870–1924): The leader of the Russian Bolsheviks, and of the Soviet Union from its inception in the Bolshevik Revolution of 1917 until his death. When Lenin was 17 years old, his eldest brother, Alexander, was arrested and hanged for participating in a terrorist bomb plot threatening the life of Czar Alexander III. Lenin was radicalized, and while a student of law he immersed himself in Marx's writings and in political activity. He was arrested in 1895 and exiled to Siberia. After 1900, he traveled widely in western and central Europe and founded the socialist newspaper *Iskra* ("The spark"). It was there that he published the essays that comprised *What Is to Be Done?* in 1901–1902. His strategy of a disciplined party of professional revolutionaries led to a split at the 1903 convention of the Russian Social Democratic Party between Lenin's Bolshevik faction and the more democratically-oriented Menshevik faction. With the outbreak of the World War in 1914, he was appalled at the propensity of socialist parties in Germany and France to support the war efforts of their respective governments. From exile in Switzerland, he urged the transformation of the "imperialist war" into a "class war," a position buttressed by *Imperialism, the Highest Stage of Capitalism* in 1916. After the Revolution of February 1917, which deposed the czar and led to a government of liberals and democratic socialists, Lenin returned to Russia. He published *State and Revolution*, which attacked democratic socialism and demanded a "dictatorship of the proletariat"—effectively, a dictatorship of the Communist Party ruling in the name of the proletariat. With the Bolshevik Revolution of October 1917, he became the leader of the new Soviet state and moved quickly to eliminate his more democratic socialist opponents.

Marcuse, Herbert (1898–1979): Born to a middle class family in Berlin. As a recently demobilized soldier at the end of the First World War, he participated in the abortive Spartacist revolution in Berlin. He studied philosophy and wrote a dissertation on Hegel with Martin Heidegger. As a leftist of Jewish origin, he departed from Germany in 1933 and moved to the United States, where he was associated with the Institute for Social Research, an independent research institution headed by Max Horkheimer that tried to combine insights from Marx and Freud into an analysis of contemporary capitalist societies. During the Second World War, Marcuse served in American intelligence agencies as an analyst of Nazi Germany, and after the war he joined the State Department as an expert on Central Europe. During the 1950s and 1960s, he taught philosophy at a series of American universities, as well as lecturing widely in France and Germany, and was regarded as an intellectual progenitor of the New Left. His book *Eros and Civilization: A Philosophical Inquiry into Freud* (1955) recast the radical critique of capitalism into the psychoanalytic language favored by American cultural elites of the age. His most influential book, *One-Dimensional Man* (1964), offered an account and critique of the ability of contemporary capitalism to keep the masses quiescent through the manipulation of their needs.

Marx, Karl (1818–1883): Marx was the son of a lawyer in the Rhineland, who hoped that Karl too would pursue a legal career. Instead Karl switched to philosophy, writing a thesis on Greek philosophy, but focusing his activity on the Young Hegelians, a loose group of thinkers who radicalized Hegel's thought in a variety of directions. Karl was attracted to atheism and to political radicalism. He moved to Paris in 1843, where he became a socialist and wrote a number of manuscripts (unpublished in his lifetime) exploring the theme of alienation under capitalism. Shortly thereafter he began his collaboration with Friedrich Engels. Together they wrote a series of works that wrestled with contemporary radical and socialist theorists and laid the basis for what became known as "historical materialism." Their key conclusions were presented in *The Communist Manifesto*, a summary and rhetorically brilliant statement of their contentions. After participating in the failed revolutions of 1848 in Germany, Marx made his way to London, where he lived for the rest of his life. He produced a steady stream of journalism (largely to aid in supporting his family), wrote a number of uncompleted works analyzing the history and nature of capitalism (including *Capital*, Volume 1, published in 1867), and founded the International Workingmen's Association to unite socialists from across Europe. He died in 1883, with most of his manuscripts unfinished. Volumes 2 and 3 of *Capital* were edited and published by Engels, and other manuscripts would be published in the half century after Marx's death.

Mises, Ludwig von (1881–1973): Born in the Austro-Hungarian Empire and raised in Vienna. As a student he was deeply influenced by the economists Carl Menger and Eugen von Böhm-Bawerk. From 1909 until his departure from Austria in 1934, he worked as an economic advisor to the Vienna Chamber of Commerce and Industry, which brought him into contact with the leading figures in Austrian commerce and government. Mises published a major work on monetary theory, *Theory of Money and Credit*, in 1912. Late in 1919, in the wake of the Bolshevik Revolution in Russia and attempts at socialist revolutions in central Europe, he wrote his most influential essay, "Economic Calculation in the Socialist Commonwealth," and in 1922 published a book-length critique of socialism, followed in 1927 by *Liberalism*, a defense of laissez-faire liberalism. Of Jewish origin (though not identification), Mises left Austria in 1934 for a post in Geneva, and then in 1940 emigrated to the United States. In 1944 he published a radical critique of virtually all forms of contemporary government, *Omnipotent Government: The Rise of the Total State and Total War*. He later taught at New York University and became a major influence on American libertarianism.

Myrdal, Gunnar (1898–1987): A prominent social democratic economist, and together with his wife Alva, a key figure in the development of the Swedish welfare state. He was Professor of Economics at the Stockholm School of Economics and simultaneously a Social Democratic member of Parliament. He coauthored with Alva Myrdal *Crisis in the Population Question* (1934), which argued that the Swedish population would decline without government measures to socialize the costs of child rearing. He is best known in the United States for his influential study of American race relations, *An American Dilemma: The Negro Problem and Modern Democracy*, originally published in 1944. In 1974, he was the cowinner of the Nobel Prize for Economics, together with his ideological rival Friedrich Hayek.

Olson, Mancur (1932–1998): An American economist who taught at Princeton and then at the University of Maryland. His work lies at the intersection of economics and political science. He made his name with the publication in 1965 of *The Logic of Collective Action: Public Goods and the Theory of Groups*, which explored the ways in which coalitions of special interests in a democracy can frustrate the efficient provision of public goods, especially competitive markets. He pursued the theme further in *The Rise and Decline of Nations: Economic Growth, Stagflation, and Social Rigidities* (1982).

Rousseau, Jean-Jacques (1712–1778): The most important internal critic of the Enlightenment. That is to say, he agreed with the Enlightenment's goal of the improvement of earthly happiness but was dubious about whether material, scientific, and technological improvement would actually make people happier. Born in Geneva, he moved to Paris in 1742, where he met Denis Diderot, the editor of the *Encyclopedia*, to which he contributed articles on music (one of his areas of expertise) and political economy. In 1749, as Rousseau was walking to visit Diderot, he was struck by the insight that remained the premise of his subsequent work—the natural goodness of humanity. The next year he published his "Discourse on the Arts and Sciences," followed in 1755 by his "Discourse on the Origin and Foundations of Inequality Among Men." In 1762, he published his greatest work of political theory, *The Social Contract*, and his highly influential novel, *Émile, or On Education*, which influenced pedagogical theory and practice for generations. Because his works were critical of Christianity (while defending a sentiment-based conception of natural religion), Rousseau was persecuted, and he moved to England in 1766, where he was aided by David Hume. But Rousseau began to suffer from delusions of paranoia, which led to a falling-out with Hume and Rousseau's eventual return to Paris. In 1794, during the French Revolution, his body was disinterred and reburied in the Pantheon, across from his rival, Voltaire.

Schmitt, Carl (1888–1985): A German Professor of Law, a political theorist of note, and one of the most distinguished intellectual supporters of the National Socialist regime. During the Weimar Republic, he published a series of works that emphasized the dysfunction of parliamentary government and explored more authoritarian alternatives. In *The Crisis of Parliamentary Democracy* (1923), he pointed to the gap between the liberal theory of representative government, based on the notion that rational discussion would produce policies in the public interest, and the reality of contemporary parliamentarianism. In *The Protector of the Constitution* (1931), he argued that parliamentary politics was incapable of providing the unity required by the state and offered as an alternative an authoritarian system headed by an elected president, ruling with the support of the civil service and the army. Though he had not been a supporter of the National Socialists before 1933, Schmitt embraced the new regime after Hitler was appointed chancellor, and provided legal reasoning for some of its most controversial and violent measures. After the Second World War, he continued to produce works of political theory as well as apologetic accounts of his own history.

Schumpeter, Joseph A. (1883–1950): One of the most wide-ranging social scientists of the first half of the 20th century. Schumpeter was born in Moravia, in what was then the Austro-Hungarian Empire, and died in the United States. In 1911, at the age of 28, he published his seminal *Theory of Economic Development* and was appointed to a Professorship of Economics. During the First World War, he was an advisor to the government of Austria-Hungary and published a refutation of Marxist theories of imperialism, "The Sociology of Imperialism." When the war ended, he served a brief stint as the finance minister of the new Austrian state, became a bank director, and then returned to academic life in Germany. In 1932, he accepted a position at Harvard University, moving to the United States just as Roosevelt became president. In 1939 he published a massive study, *Business Cycles: A Theoretical, Historical and Statistical Analysis of the Capitalist Process*, followed by *Capitalism, Socialism and Democracy* (1942), which was written for a wider audience. His erudite *History of Economic Analysis* was published posthumously in 1954.

Simmel, Georg (1858–1918): An academic who ranged freely between philosophy, sociology, economics, history, and religion. Born near the commercial epicenter of Berlin, he lived most of his life in the capital. As an unorthodox academic with an independent income, he was able to transcend disciplinary boundaries and reach a large audience without holding an academic chair. His book *The Philosophy of Money* began as an 1889 lecture on "The Psychology of Money" and ended as an amalgam of history, philosophy, sociology, and social psychology. Its emphasis on the rationalizing effects of a money economy influenced the subsequent conceptualization of capitalism by Max Weber and Werner Sombart. His *Sociology* (1908) was a major contribution to the analysis of social structure and influenced American sociology, including Robert K. Merton's social role theory. Among Simmel's best-known essays are "The Stranger," "The Web of Group-Affiliations," and "The Metropolis and Mental Life."

Smith, Adam (1723–1790): Smith was born in Kirkcaldy, Scotland, and attended the University of Glasgow and then Oxford University. In 1748 he moved to Edinburgh, where he lectured on the history of belles lettres. In 1751, at the age of 27, he was appointed to a professorship at the University of Glasgow, first in logic and then in moral philosophy. In 1759 he published the first edition of *The Theory of Moral Sentiments*, one of the great works of Enlightenment thought, which presented an explanation of how conscience is formed by interaction with others and by the mind's desire for the approval first of others and then of self-approval. In the years thereafter, he lectured on political economy until he was hired away by a Scottish nobleman to accompany his stepson on a trip to the Continent. Smith then moved to London, where he wrote *The*

Wealth of Nations, published in 1776. Having long served as an advisor to politicians, he was appointed as a commissioner of customs for Scotland, so he spent most of the years after the publication of his masterwork as a civil servant. He returned to the concerns of his first book, publishing a substantially revised sixth edition of the *Theory of Moral Sentiments* in 1790, the year of his death. Smith also worked on a treatise on government but never completed it to his satisfaction. Its contents have come down to us through the notes taken by his students at Glasgow and published as the *Lectures on Jurisprudence*.

Sombart, Werner (1863–1941): Sombart was an economic historian whose works raised provocative questions much superior to the quality of his answers. Like his contemporary Max Weber, he studied law and economics, and he was among the founders of sociology in Germany. In 1917 he was appointed to the chair of economics at the University of Berlin. Among his most important works were a multivolume history of capitalism (1902–1927); a 1906 essay, "Why is There No Socialism in the United States?" which contributed to an ongoing debate about American exceptionalism; and his 1911 book, *The Jews and Modern Capitalism*. Sombart began as a sympathizer of Marxist socialism, but his increasing nationalism led him to move to the right, and he ended up a somewhat ambivalent supporter of national socialism.

Tocqueville, Alexis de (1805–1859): The scion of a noble French family, de Tocqueville chose a career in law and politics. Believing that democracy was the wave of the future, and that the United States was the purest existing democratic nation, he managed to be sent to America to study its penal system. From April 1831 through February 1832, he traveled across much of the United States, meeting with statesmen as well as more common folk, before returning to France and publishing the first volume of *Democracy in America* in 1835; the second volume, more speculative in nature, followed five years later. De Tocqueville was active in French political life, and after the fall of the July Monarchy during the February 1848 Revolution, he was elected a member of the Constituent Assembly of 1848, where he became a member of the Commission charged with the drafting of the new Constitution of the Second Republic. With mounting anxiety, he experienced the radicalization of the revolution and supported its repression by General Cavaignac, an experience described in his posthumously published *Recollections*. An opponent of Louis Bonaparte, who came to power in 1851 and adopted the title of Emperor Napoleon III, de Tocqueville retired to his chateau, where he wrote *The Old Regime and the French Revolution* (1856), one of the most influential analyses of modern French history.

Tönnies, Friedrich (1855–1936): One of the founders of sociology in Germany. Influenced by Hobbes, Marx, and romantic nationalists such as Paul de Lagarde, Tönnies synthesized their thoughts in *Community and Society* (1887), a work that set the terms for debates on capitalism in German thought. He later wrote on a wide range of sociological topics, including public opinion and the changing means of communication. In imperial Germany, he was denied a professorship until 1913 because of his leftist sympathies and was later ousted from his post as emeritus professor by the Nazis.

Weber, Max (1864–1920): Weber was trained in the law, but from early on his interests were as much economic, historical, and sociological as legal. His doctoral thesis was on the history of medieval business organizations, and in 1891 he completed the second dissertation required to teach at a German university on Roman agrarian history. In 1896 he became Professor of Political Economy at the University of Heidelberg. While he continued to live in that town for most of his adult life, he retired from active teaching in 1899 because of an emotional disorder that kept him from regular scholarly activity. He marked his recovery with the publication in 1904–1905 of his essay "The Protestant Ethic and the 'Spirit' of Capitalism." The essay set off a controversy about the connections between religion and capitalist economic development that included Werner Sombart, among many others. In an effort to extend the range of his analysis, Weber pursued a number of subsequent studies on the economic ethics of world religions. The relationships between social and economic life were also at the center of *Economy and Society*, a work published posthumously in 1923.

Bibliography

Essential Primary Sources

Buchanan, James. "Keynesian Economics in Democratic Politics." In *Democracy in Deficit: The Political Legacy of Lord Keynes*, 95–109. Indianapolis, IN: Liberty Fund, 2000. Presents Buchanan's most succinct critique of Keynesianism.

———. *The Logical Foundations of Constitutional Liberty*. Indianapolis, IN: Liberty Fund, 1999. A seminal statement of public choice theory.

Burke, Edmund. *Reflections on the Revolution in France: A Critical Edition*. Edited by J. C. D. Clark. Stanford, CA: Stanford University Press, 2001. Perhaps the best available edition of this most influential work of conservative analysis, heavily annotated and with a long introduction by the editor.

Clark, Henry C., ed. *Commerce, Culture and Liberty: Readings on Capitalism before Adam Smith*. Indianapolis, IN: Liberty Fund, 2003. A very useful collection of readings from 17th- and 18th-century European authors, including Barbon, Mandeville, Voltaire, and Rousseau.

Collini, Stefan, ed. *Arnold: Culture and Anarchy and Other Writings*. Cambridge: Cambridge University Press, 1993. Includes Arnold's most important essays of cultural criticism.

Crosland, C. A. R. *The Future of Socialism*. New York: Schocken, 1956. An influential work in redefining socialism in the direction of welfare-state capitalism.

De Tocqueville, Alexis. *See* Tocqueville, Alexis de.

Gellner, Ernest. *Nations and Nationalism*. Ithaca, NY: Cornell University Press, 1983. Gellner's non-Marxist historical materialist analysis argues that the rise of nationalism is inextricably linked to capitalist economic development (what he calls "industrial society").

Hamilton, Alexander. *Report on the Subject of Manufactures*. Widely available online. The remarkable analysis and program of economic development by America's first secretary of the treasury.

Hayek, Friedrich A. *Individualism and Economic Order*. Chicago: University of Chicago Press, 1948. Includes Hayek's 1935 contributions to the "socialist calculation debate" as well as his seminal essay "The Use of Knowledge in Society."

———. *The Mirage of Social Justice*. Chicago: University of Chicago Press, 1976. Hayek's most incisive critique of some of the philosophical premises of the welfare state, including his critique of "equality of opportunity," plus a discussion of his distinction between the tribal and great societies.

———. *The Road to Serfdom*. Edited by Bruce Caldwell. Chicago: University of Chicago Press, 2007. Originally published in 1944, this wide-ranging work has long been Hayek's best-known book. It is also his most polemical. This new edition includes useful supplementary material and an introduction by the editor dealing with the genesis and impact of the book.

Hegel, G. W. F. *Elements of the Philosophy of Right*. Edited by Allen W. Wood. Cambridge: Cambridge University Press, 1991. The most important of Hegel's works, for his views on capitalism.

Hobbes, Thomas. *Leviathan*. Edited, with introduction and notes, by Edwin Curley. Indianapolis, IN: Hackett Publishing, 1994. The most useful available edition of what is perhaps the greatest work of philosophy in the English language, with modernized spelling.

Hobson, J. A. *Imperialism*. Published in 1902; available online. An influential critique of imperialism from a radical British liberal.

Kaes, Anton, et al. *The Weimar Republic Sourcebook*. Berkeley: University of California Press, 1994. An anthology of work from the Weimar Republic that includes selections from Freyer and Schmitt as well as others.

Lenin, V. I. *What Is to Be Done?* Edited by Robert Service. New York: Penguin, 1988. Lenin's most important revision of Marxism.

Marcuse, Herbert. *One-Dimensional Man*. Boston: Beacon Press, 1964. Marcuse's most influential critique of contemporary capitalism.

Marx, Karl. *Capital, Volume 1*. Translated by Ben Fowkes. New York: Penguin Classics, 1990. The only volume of *Capital* published in Marx's lifetime; in a modern translation, with a wide-ranging if uncritical introduction by Marxist economist Ernest Mandel.

Marx, Karl, and Friedrich Engels. *The Communist Manifesto*. Edited by John E. Toews. Boston: Bedford, 1999. This edition comes with a well-informed introduction by the editor and some illuminating excerpts from other works by Marx and Engels.

Mises, Ludwig von. *Economic Calculation in the Socialist Commonwealth*. Translated by S. Adler. Published in 1920. Available online at http://mises.org/pdf/econcalc.pdf. A prescient critique of socialism, with implications for understanding capitalism as well.

Olson, Mancur. *The Logic of Collective Action: Public Goods and the Theory of Groups*. Cambridge, MA: Harvard University Press, 1971. A succinct exploration of how committed minorities can exercise influence out of proportion to their numbers.

———. *The Rise and Decline of Nations: Economic Growth, Stagflation, and Social Rigidities*. New Haven, CT: Yale University Press, 1982. A book that draws out some of the implications of Olson's earlier work to account for economic stagnation.

Rousseau, Jean-Jacques. *Rousseau: The Discourses and Other Early Political Writings*. Edited and translated by Victor Gourevitch. Cambridge: Cambridge University Press, 1997. A wonderful edition of Rousseau's first and second discourses, together with supplementary materials and a fine introduction.

Schmitt, Carl. "When Parliament Cannot Be Sovereign." In Muller, *Conservatism*, 261–74. A succinct statement of some of Schmitt's key analyses of the Weimar polity.

Schumpeter, Joseph A. *Capitalism, Socialism and Democracy*. New York: Harper and Row, 1942. Schumpeter's wide-ranging summa. Eminently readable, despite many stylistic Germanicisms. Later editions include an introduction by Tom Bottomore, which is best ignored.

———. *The Economics and Sociology of Capitalism*. Edited by Richard Swedberg. Princeton, NJ: Princeton University Press, 1991. This collection includes a number of seminal essays, including "The Crisis of the Tax State," "The Sociology of Imperialism," and "Social Classes in an Ethnically Homogeneous Environment." There is a long and informed introduction by the editor.

———. *Essays on Entrepreneurs, Innovations, Business Cycles, and the Evolution of Capitalism*. Edited by Richard V. Clemence. New Brunswick, NJ: Transaction Books, 1989. A collection of Schumpeter's essays, which complement his book-length works.

———. *The Theory of Economic Development*. Translated by Redvers Opie. New Brunswick, NJ: Transaction Books, 1983. Schumpeter's pathbreaking work, much of it quite accessible.

Simmel, Georg. *Conflict and the Web of Group-Affiliations*. New York: Free Press, 1955. Two separate essays by Simmel, both highly original and pertinent for thinking about capitalism—and much else.

———. *The Philosophy of Money*. 2nd ed. Edited by David Frisby. London: Routledge, 1990. One of the richest works on capitalism ever written, but Simmel's wide range of historical and intellectual references make it a demanding work. Luckily, one need not grasp every argument to profit from the book's insights—if there is something you don't understand, just push on.

Smith, Adam. *An Inquiry into the Nature and Causes of the Wealth of Nations*. Edited by R. H. Campbell and A. S. Skinner. Indianapolis, IN: Liberty Classics, 1981. The best edition of Smith's classic work, with footnotes that illuminate the text.

Tocqueville, Alexis de. *Democracy in America*. Translated by Arthur Goldhammer. New York: Library of America, 2004. Of the half a dozen English translations of this work, this is the most readable and reliable, and it includes an extensive chronology and translator's notes that illuminate the text.

Voltaire. *Letters on England*. Translated by Leonard Tancock. New York: Penguin, 1980. Among Voltaire's earliest and most effective works of criticism, shot through with political arguments for commerce.

Weber, Max. *The Protestant Ethic and the "Spirit" of Capitalism and Other Writings*. Edited and translated by Peter Baehr and Gordon C. Wells. New York: Penguin, 2002. The first English translation of the original 1905 text, together with Weber's later rejoinders to his critics. Better in most respects than the earlier translation by Talcott Parsons of the 1920 version of the text.

Williams, David, ed. *Voltaire: Political Writings*. Cambridge: Cambridge University Press, 1994. A useful selection, including Voltaire's views on economy, finance, and taxes.

Secondary Works on Particular Thinkers

Avineri, Shlomo. *Hegel's Theory of the Modern State*. Cambridge: Cambridge University Press, 1972. An informed and accessible introduction to a difficult thinker.

Elster, John. *An Introduction to Karl Marx*. Cambridge: Cambridge University Press, 1986. A re-creation and critique of Marx's key contentions.

Evensky, Jerry. *Adam Smith's Moral Philosophy: A Contemporary Perspective on Markets, Law, Ethics and Culture.* Cambridge: Cambridge University Press, 2005. An accessible discussion of Smith's work and its contemporary implications, written by an economist.

Fleischacker, Samuel. *On Adam Smith's "Wealth of Nations": A Philosophical Companion.* Princeton, NJ: Princeton University Press, 2004. A well-informed and wide-ranging examination of the philosophical arguments and underpinnings of *The Wealth of Nations*, which stresses Smith's egalitarian propensities.

Frisby, David. *Georg Simmel.* New York: Tavistock, 1984. An overview of a multifaceted thinker.

Jay, Martin. *The Dialectical Imagination: A History of the Frankfurt School and the Institute for Social Research, 1923–1950.* Boston: Little, Brown, 1973. A clear and wide-ranging reconstruction of the thinkers with whom Marcuse was most closely associated.

Malcolm, Noel. *Aspects of Hobbes.* Oxford: Oxford University Press, 2002. Explorations of Hobbes's life, thought, and influence by a leading contemporary scholar.

McCraw, Thomas K. *Prophet of Innovation: Joseph Schumpeter and Creative Destruction.* Cambridge, MA: Harvard University Press, 2007. An accessible account of Schumpeter's life and thought, with an emphasis on his theory of innovation and on his American period.

McNamara, Peter. *Statesmanship and Political Economy: Smith, Hamilton, and the Foundation of the Commercial Republic.* DeKalb: Northern Illinois University Press, 1998. This book explores Hamilton's divergence from Smith, not only on matters of policy but on the way in which politicians should think about economic matters.

Muller, Jerry Z. *Adam Smith in His Time and Ours: Designing the Decent Society.* Princeton, NJ: Princeton University Press, 1995. An introduction to Smith's life, context, and thought, with an emphasis on Smith as a public policy analyst, and the common conceptual foundations of *The Theory of Moral Sentiments* and *The Wealth of Nations*.

———. *Conservatism: An Anthology of Social and Political Thought from David Hume to the Present.* Princeton, NJ: Princeton University Press, 1997. Introduction, Afterword, and selections from Burke. An exploration of the nature of conservative thought and Burke's place in it.

Muthu, Sankar. "Adam Smith's Critique of International Trading Companies: Theorizing 'Globalization' in the Age of Enlightenment." *Political Theory* 36 (April 2008): 185–212. An extended discussion of Smith's critique of the East India Company.

Oakeshott, Michael. *Hobbes on Civil Association*. Indianapolis, IN: Liberty Fund, 1975. An illuminating exploration of the premises, arguments, and implications of Hobbes's *Leviathan* by a major 20th-century political philosopher.

O'Brien, Conor Cruise. *The Great Melody: A Thematic Biography of Edmund Burke*. Chicago: University of Chicago Press, 1992. An extended and informed discussion of Burke's critique of the East India Company.

Pinkard, Terry. *Hegel: A Biography*. Cambridge: Cambridge University Press, 2000. The best biography of Hegel; explores his ideas as well.

Schleifer, James T. *The Making of Tocqueville's Democracy in America*. 2nd ed. Indianapolis, IN: Liberty Fund, 2000. Explores the intellectual sources from which Tocqueville drew in writing his great work, and the uses he made of them.

Walker, Mack. *German Home Towns: Community, State, and General Estate 1648–1871*. Ithaca, NY: Cornell University Press, 1971. A brilliant re-creation of the political, economic, and cultural context of Möser's world.

Welch, Cheryl B., ed. *The Cambridge Companion to Tocqueville*. Cambridge: Cambridge University Press, 2006. An informed exploration of various facets of de Tocqueville's life and work.

Works on the History of Thinking about the Market

Berman, Sheri. *The Primacy of Politics: Social Democracy and the Making of Europe's Twentieth Century*. Cambridge: Cambridge University Press, 2006. A sympathetic presentation of the development of social democracy as a mode of thought distinct from traditional socialism.

Degler, Carl N. *At Odds: Women and the Family in America from the Revolution to the Present*. New York: Oxford University Press, 1980. A wide-ranging survey of the history of the family in America.

Goldin, Claudia. "The Quiet Revolution That Transformed Women's Employment, Education, and Family." *AEA Papers and Proceedings*

19 (May 2006): 1–21. An important essay, including a discussion of the economic effects of the birth control pill.

Hirschman, Albert O. *The Passions and the Interests: Political Arguments for Capitalism before Its Triumph.* Twentieth Anniversary ed. Princeton, NJ: Princeton University Press, 1997. A now classic exploration of 17th- and 18th-century arguments about capitalism.

———. *Rival Views of Market Society and Other Recent Essays.* New York: Viking, 1986. The title essay of this collection is a penetrating schematic analysis of arguments for and against the market. Other included essays related to the theme of the market are "The Concept of Interest: From Euphemism to Tautology" and "Exit and Voice: An Expanding Sphere of Influence."

Hont, Istvan. *Jealousy of Trade: International Competition and the Nation-State in Historical Perspective.* Cambridge, MA: Harvard University Press, 2005. An erudite collection of essays exploring the arguments for and against economic nationalism (and much else) in the 18th century.

Irwin, Douglas A. *Against the Tide: An Intellectual History of Free Trade.* Princeton, NJ: Princeton University Press, 1996. An accessible overview of the arguments for and against free trade from the 17th to the 20th century.

Kolakowski, Leszek. *Main Currents of Marxism.* 3 vols. New York: Oxford University Press, 1978. Reprinted in a single volume by Norton, 2008. The best history of Marxist thought, though weaker on its economic elements.

Mommsen, Wolfgang A. *Theories of Imperialism.* Translated by P. S. Falla. New York: Random House, 1980. A useful survey.

Muller, Jerry Z. *The Mind and the Market: Capitalism in Modern European Thought.* New York: Knopf, 2002. An exploration of many of the European thinkers dealt with in this course, placing them in their economic, cultural, and political contexts.

Noonan, John T. *The Scholastic Analysis of Usury.* Cambridge, MA: Harvard University Press, 1957. A learned exposition of the history of Catholic thinking about economic matters.

Rahe, Paul. *Republics Ancient and Modern.* Vol. 1, *The Ancien Regime in Classical Greece.* Chapel Hill: University of North Carolina Press, 1994. A historically informed exploration of the centrality of martial virtue to the survival of the Greek city-states and therefore of its centrality to classical republicanism, as opposed to the more commercial republicanism that arose in the early modern era.

Viner, Jacob. *Essays on the Intellectual History of Economics.* Edited by Douglas A. Irwin. Princeton, NJ: Princeton University Press, 1991. Valuable studies of mercantilist thought and Adam Smith, and a searching critique of Hayek.

Works on the History of Capitalism

Anderson, Benedict. *Imagined Communities: Reflections on the Origins and Spread of Nationalism.* Rev. ed. London: Verso, 1991. Offers an interpretation of the links between capitalism and nationalism with different emphases from Gellner's theory.

Bell, Daniel. *The Coming of Post-Industrial Society: A Venture in Social Forecasting.* New York: Basic Books, 1973. Twentieth anniversary edition with a new forward, 1999. A prescient and influential characterization of the changing character of capitalism. Most of its main theses are articulated in the forward to the new edition.

———. *The Cultural Contradictions of Capitalism.* New York: Basic Books, 1976. Part I, "The Double Bind of Modernity," lays out Bell's arguments about the ways in which contemporary capitalism seemed to undermine capitalism itself.

Braudel, Fernand. *Civilization and Capitalism, 15th–18th Century.* 3 vols. Translated by Sian Reynolds. New York: Harper and Row, 1982. A sprawling, conceptually weak but empirically rich account of early modern capitalism.

Chandler, Alfred D. Jr., Franco Amatori, and Takashi Hikino, eds. *Big Business and the Wealth of Nations.* Cambridge: Cambridge University Press, 1997. A collection that applies and extends internationally the analysis of the rise of the large corporation first explored in Chandler's *The Visible Hand: The Managerial Revolution in American Business* (1980).

De Vries, Jan. *The Industrious Revolution: Consumer Behavior and the Household Economy, 1650 to the Present.* Cambridge: Cambridge University Press, 2008. An exploration of the interaction of the family and the market, making use of the tools of the economist as well as those of the historian.

Frieden, Jeffry A. *Global Capitalism: Its Fall and Rise in the Twentieth Century*. New York: Norton, 2006. An excellent overview and analysis of the last hundred years of economic history.

Landes, David S. *The Unbound Prometheus: Technological Change and Industrial Development in Western Europe from 1750 to the Present*. Cambridge: Cambridge University Press, 1969. A classic account of the history of European industrialization. Its attention to culture and society means that it delivers more than the subtitle promises.

———. *The Wealth and Poverty of Nations: Why Some Are So Rich and Some Are So Poor*. New York: Norton, 1998. A leading economic historian with a feel for culture and institutions explores one of the biggest historical questions.

Lopez, Robert S. *The Commercial Revolution of the Middle Ages, 950–1350*. Cambridge: Cambridge University Press, 1976. A now classic account of what one might call the prehistory of modern capitalism.

McCraw, Thomas K., ed. *Creating Modern Capitalism: How Entrepreneurs, Companies, and Countries Triumphed in Three Industrial Revolutions*. Cambridge, MA: Harvard University Press, 1997. Studies of some of the most influential entrepreneurs and corporations in Britain, Germany, Japan, and the United States, from the 18th to the 20th century, which help to bring out the varieties of capitalism.

Some Notable Works of Contemporary Analysis

Bannock, Graham, et al. *The Penguin Dictionary of Economics*. 7th ed. New York: Penguin, 2003. A useful book to have at hand when reading about economic matters.

Baumol, William J., Robert E. Litan, and Carl J. Schramm. *Good Capitalism, Bad Capitalism and the Economics of Growth and Prosperity*. New Haven, CT: Yale University Press, 2007. An accessible analysis of the varieties of contemporary capitalism and the role of entrepreneurship in economic growth.

Bhidé, Amar. *The Venturesome Economy: How Innovation Sustains Prosperity in an Interconnected World*. Princeton, NJ: Princeton University Press, 2008. A leading student of entrepreneurial innovation explores contemporary economic developments with a focus on businesses backed by American venture capital. A wide-ranging book dealing with innovation, offshoring and its limits in a service economy, immigration, and the advantages of the international division of labor.

Chang, Ha-Joon. *Bad Samaritans: The Myth of Free Trade and the Secret History of Capitalism*. New York: Bloomsbury Press, 2008. A bracing critique of the reigning "Washington consensus" on liberalization and globalization. The book argues that historically, countries have successfully integrated into the global economy through various protectionist policies, and that contemporary developing countries ought to do so as well. A one-sided polemical work, but a useful counter to some of the other works listed in this section.

Cowen, Tyler. *Creative Destruction: How Globalization is Changing the World's Cultures*. Princeton, NJ: Princeton University Press, 2002. This book applies a "gains from trade" model to understand international cultural exchange and argues that "just as trade typically makes countries richer in material terms, it tends to make them culturally richer as well."

Esping-Andersen, Gøsta. *Social Foundations of Postindustrial Economies*. New York: Oxford University Press, 1999. A difficult but insightful exploration of the links between welfare regimes, markets, and family patterns.

Friedman, Thomas L. *The Lexus and the Olive Tree: Understanding Globalization*. Expanded edition. New York: Anchor, 2000. An accessible introduction to contemporary globalization and its discontents.

Muller, Jerry Z. "Us and Them: The Enduring Power of Ethnic Nationalism." *Foreign Affairs*, March/April 2008, 18–35. Also available online. Provides a narrative of the effects of ethnic nationalism on 20th-century Europe.

Notes